A
LIFE
LIVED

A
LIFE
LIVED

Liz Parker

The Book Guild Ltd

First published in Great Britain in 2017 by
The Book Guild Ltd
9 Priory Business Park
Wistow Road, Kibworth
Leicestershire, LE8 0RX
Freephone: 0800 999 2982
www.bookguild.co.uk
Email: info@bookguild.co.uk
Twitter: @bookguild

Typeset in Minion Pro

Printed and bound in the UK by TJ International, Padstow, Cornwall

ISBN 9781911320593

British Library Cataloguing in Publication Data.
A catalogue record for this book is available from the British Library.

For Fiona, Simon, Claire, Ben and Joe

"All the world's a stage,
And all the men and women merely players;
They have their exits and their entrances;..."

W. Shakespeare, *As You Like It*

PROLOGUE

The Ancient Athenians believed that an owl brought wisdom, but the western world believes that it is a harbinger of death.

I had this experience of finding a dead owl in my house after returning from a long absence. It was lying on the floor in the living room; there were no windows open so it must have fallen down the chimney. It had not been dead for long, and there was no smell.

Why am I telling you this? At that time I did not think of the significance of the portent, I just got on with clearing it away in a plastic bag and throwing it into the field behind my Greek house where it would rot down or be devoured by the wild cats.

Then the most tragic event of my life occurred about three months after finding the dead owl. Now, when I hear the owl's eerie cry in the night, I weep.

LIZZIE - THE MOTHER

ACT I

I am a mother. I never had an overwhelming urge to have children. In fact, in the 1950s, after I had lost my virginity, I procured a Dutch cap (there were no contraceptive pills then). I might as well have worn the cap on my head for the protection it gave me! Several illegal abortions later and during my first marriage, I gave birth to two beautiful healthy daughters; then, during my second marriage, I produced a long awaited, gorgeous son. They all had the requisite fingers and toes. My children became my reason for being.

I was born in India. My father, a handsome, small but dynamic civil engineer and tea planter, had gone on leave to England and during that time he had paid a visit to my mother (whom he knew before leaving for India) in order to pay his condolences since she had lost her first husband after six months of marriage due to pneumonia. My father fell for my mother, but he had to return to India. He continued to woo her with long letters. His writing was very small, so he must have been able to write much needed information in his missives. Father proposed by post and mother accepted.

Several months later my mother, alone, embarked on a passenger liner from Southampton, for the arduous trip to Calcutta. What were her thoughts? Perhaps she was hoping to leave her lower middle class background and find adventure and excitement in the mystical East. Tales of the hedonistic lifestyle in India could have beguiled her, but she was sailing to spend her life with a man she hardly knew. Mother was slim and attractive, with an aquiline profile and huge hazel eyes that would fill with tears when she laughed. She laughed a lot. Certainly she would have had many suitors in England – she chose to seek a new experience in the land of the Raj.

They married in 1929. I have a sepia photograph of them taken on that

1

day. My mother did not look very happy, nor did my father or the two others in the photo, but in those days one did not smile for the photographer. However, she should have had plenty to smile about. They lived on a large tea estate in Sylhet, which was then Assam, in a huge bungalow with servants galore: bearers who waited at table, gardeners, cleaning women, cooks and my Ayah, the equivalent of an English Nanny. The English Club was where my mother spent a lot of her time, playing tennis, cards and drinking gin and tonic (this was recommended for health reasons because the quinine in the tonic kept the dreaded mosquitoes at bay!). My father excelled at polo and owned several ponies; he cut a very dashing figure in his jodhpurs and their life must have been idyllic.

My sister, Jean, was born four years before me. She looked like a little Indian girl, very dark and pretty and impish with a cheeky smile. I was born in 1934, on the 17th of October – a Libran. My mother had journeyed to the cooler area of Shillong, in the foothills of the Himalayas to await my birth. However, although my delivery was straightforward, I was a sickly child. I had blonde hair, a pale skin and contracted dysentery when very young. I survived that illness. Later, I was told, I was rescued from certain death by my Ayah when a deadly snake dropped from the bamboo ceiling into my playpen. My attentive Ayah snatched me to safety as I crawled toward the new plaything!

The imminent threat of war in 1938 forced my parents to review the future. In those days there was no schooling for children of white colonials in India. My sister had a governess and attended the only inferior local education facility nearby. My parents decided that we must return to England for a proper education. My father had a female friend from university who ran a small school in Cornwall. We could board there and she would be our guardian. The necessary arrangements for travel were made. It was decided, that, my mother, my sister and I were to sail to England. My father had to stay in India because of his work. I do not have any real recollection of the voyage, except perhaps the rails of the ship. I think, now, about what this departure must have meant to my Ayah, to have a four-year-old child taken from her, a child who she had nurtured from birth, a little soul whom she loved. She had probably left her own children with her mother because she needed the money to survive and had to find work elsewhere. I was *her* child.

I believe a spiritual transference was created between us. I imagine her

2

holding me in her arms, murmuring her mantras and saying her Hindu prayers as she smiled down at me. Is this the reason that I did not feel I belonged in a Western society? Why I have searched all my life to find that safe place with a spiritual connection? The closest I have come is by becoming a Buddhist – and not a very good one either – but the philosophy of Buddhism appeals to me and connects me to my Indian roots and to my surrogate mother, who I never saw again.

I was four years old when I went to boarding school. My sister became my loving carer and confidant. I knew my mother had to return to India and the head mistress of the school, my father's friend, was attentive and tried to understand the loss we girls felt at being motherless – but despite being brought up in the wild, beautiful and peaceful countryside of Cornwall during the war years, I felt an increasing need within my being to replace my lack of parenting with something that I could control, a way of life that was of my choosing and which brought me satisfaction. I thought I found a way.

There was never any doubt in my mind that I wanted to be an actress. It had nothing to do with the fact that my grandfather had been a stage carpenter or that my father had briefly been carried onto the boards as a screaming baby in a Victorian melodrama. The deciding factor was seeing *Gone with the Wind*, when I was twelve years old. I identified with both the character of Scarlet O'Hara and the actress Vivien Leigh. I remember snuggling into my seat and being transported into a world of make believe. I created a fantasy world, spending all my pocket money at the cinema watching frivolous extravaganzas such as *The Ziegfield Follies*. Oh! I had to be part of that world; I too would be a star.

The all-girl boarding school I attended for twelve years specialised in music. However, I associated the learning of scales and music with numbers, because I was innumerate (and still am). I failed to achieve any coordination on the piano, violin or cello. I suggested to my careworn headmistress and guardian that I should study elocution instead. Miss Bentley almost sighed with relief as she agreed and I skipped out of her office, knowing that my future plan to be a thespian would be enhanced by learning to speak properly. I excelled in all my Guildhall Exams and produced *Julius Caesar* for the school drama competition. All the roles were played by girls. It was a bit like Shakespearian times, only in reverse! However, the strict upbringing did not quell my rebellious spirit and

I became the ringleader of my year. Every day we would go for a walk accompanied by some weary teacher. The school was in the town of Seaford, a bleak place in Sussex, and near the dangerous and sheer cliffs of Beachy Head, where many people chose to commit suicide. One afternoon, Miss Fortescue had taken our class for a nature ramble near the edge of these cliffs. I briefed the others in my class and, while Miss Fortescue was looking away from us, we all dropped to the ground, hidden by the long grass. Miss Fortescue turned back to draw our attention to some rare sample of cuckoo spit, to discover that her charges had disappeared! She ran to the edge of the cliff, screaming and crying, threw herself on to her knees, clasping her hands in supplication.

"Oh God! Why has this happened to me? I'll never get another job again."

At this point I felt sorry for her and signalled the other miscreants to stand up.

"*Coo-ee*! Miss Fortescue, did you wonder where we were?"

The colour came back into her ravaged face and the state of shock turned to anger.

"You little devils! Who was responsible for this?"

My loyal friends said nothing, but later in Miss Bentley's office, threatened with expulsion, the finger of guilt pointed clearly at me.

"Elizabeth, if I were not your guardian I would expel you – but, because your parents are in India, I will have to find another punishment."

I was made to learn a whole chapter of *David Copperfield*! At the time I resented the severe sentence, but now I realise Miss Bentley did me a great favour. As an actress I spent many hard but enjoyable years working in weekly repertory where I had to learn my lines for a new play whilst acting in the current one. I developed a photographic memory as I studied late into the night – I would turn the pages over in my mind.

What my school and Miss Bentley did not prepare me for were *boys*. Seaford had about ten boys' schools nearby, but we were not allowed to talk or to meet any of them. The only male figures I was in contact with were my tennis coach – who I was in love with – and our biology master. For some extraordinary ill-conceived reason the headmistress thought it appropriate to have a male to teach giggling, pubescent girls this most intimate subject. Mr Bumble never dared approach the essential facts of reproduction. If we ever asked a question on this matter he would blush and say, "Ah, we will cover that next week." But he never did, with the result that the only girl who passed her Biology O Levels was a doctors' daughter! Sex and men were a mystery; the senior girls were eventually given a talk by an androgynous person regarding our expected periods and the act of coitus. She drew diagrams on the blackboard, but there was not a penis in sight, so we all thought we would have an immaculate conception! She gave us all one hammock-like sanitary towel and an elastic belt, and then disappeared, leaving us baffled and still ignorant.

I started my period late, aged fourteen. Because my parents were abroad, I would spend the holidays with whichever friend had asked me. At that traumatic time I was staying on a farm in the wilds of Sussex. My friend was not one of my closest mates and when I started to bleed, I didn't dare tell her. I found my one sanitary towel and wore it for two days. When I realised it was becoming unhygienic and uncomfortable, I stole a wodge of cotton wool from her mother's bathroom. I did not know what to do with the offending blood-stained article. Then I had an idea. Feeling like a murderer, I awoke in the middle of the night and stealthily crept out of the house to a stagnant pond that was near the house; there I hurled the offending object into the distance and tiptoed back to my bedroom. Next morning I nonchalantly wandered to the pond to ensure the bloody thing had gone – but horrors! It was hanging from the branch of a tree for all the farmhands to see. I burst into tears and ran to my girlfriend's mother. She was very sympathetic and immediately drove me to the nearest town where she bought copious supplies of sanitary towels. I never told my girlfriend. She was a bookish type and hadn't yet been "cursed".

I was sixteen when I auditioned for the Royal Academy of Dramatic Art. I had by then grown into quite an attractive teenager: dark-haired, green-eyed, with a slim figure and shapely legs. I would practice expressions in front of the mirror for hours: the vamp, the coquette, the orphan, the aristocrat.

I hid my mother's photo albums; she had returned from India but still lived in the colonial past. Mother would produce the photos to explain to her new friends what life had been like on a tea plantation and would point at the pictures of skeletal me.

"You see, that's what happened to poor Elizabeth after dysentery. Isn't she a sorrowful mess?"

"Not now, Mother dear! Now I'm a gorgeous, desirable, talented actress."

Positive thinking helped me to overcome my shyness; the plain waif exited backstage and a new, confident me entered centre stage.

I passed the audition to the RADA. I was terrified as I climbed the stone steps that led from Gower Street into the famous building. There were about a hundred other aspiring actresses waiting. I glanced at them and they all seemed to be prettier and better dressed than me, but when they called out my name, Elizabeth Howgego (I changed that surname with my first job!) I thought of Vivien Leigh. "Fiddle Dee Dee," I said and marched in front of the examining panel. Sir Kenneth Barnes, the president, was a large, genial looking man sitting in the centre of a semi-circle of imposing actors and actresses who were to be my judges; I had to wait for a torturous month for the results. I was in! But not yet. The RADA was the most prestigious drama school at that time and it was full. They recommended that I attend the Preparatory Academy in Highgate for at least two terms, until there was a vacancy.

London in the sixties was the most exciting city in the world. After the stringent conservative period of the fifties, there emerged a vibrant, bold spirited young generation who invented a new culture in England. Music, art, fashion, dance, theatre and the cinema were unique and it transformed the youth culture, attitudes towards sexual freedom and the rights of an individual to be who they wanted to be, to wear what they wanted to wear. A new "cool", confident, exuberant generation came into existence. I was going to live in that swinging town, to study, work and play with some of the most charismatic and famous personalities of the decade.

In retrospect, I was not in awe of the actors I met, like Peter O'Toole, James Villiers, Albert Finney and Timothy West, because they were all students like me. It wasn't until I married Ronald Fraser and became part of his set, which included characters like Richard Burton, Sean Connery, Paul Daneman, Judi Dench, Richard Harris, John Neville and Robert Shaw, and subsequently met the really great, established stars that I would pinch myself and think, "Is this really happening to me? This plain, shy girl from India?" God, wherever he or she was, had definitely heard my childhood prayers.

My proud, but naïve parents had obviously never heard the famous Noel Coward song, 'Don't put your daughter on the stage, Mrs Worthington...' They cheerfully waved goodbye as the train left for London, the wildest capitol in the world.

The only person I knew in the big city was my sister. Jean was a nurse, training at Great Ormond Street, the famous children's Hospital, which was conveniently across Russell Square from the RADA. During my time as a penniless student, I would eke out my pittance of a grant by dressing as a nurse, with a cape round my shoulders, and eat at the hospital canteen. But, I was going to live in Highgate at the PARADA and needed a place to stay. The registrar had found me a cheap bedsit near the college. It was a dump and miniscule: there was one bed, one wardrobe, one gas ring and lino on the floor. The landlady was Gestapo-trained, and she instructed me immediately about the rules of her prison. I was not allowed any men in my room, and if I was not back by 10.30 pm, I would be locked out!

Luckily on my first day at college I met many kindred spirits, most of them were also looking for digs. A young man called Brian Charteris, who seemed to know his way around London, told me of an available room in a huge house in Highgate where other students lived and where there was no curfew. I befriended a girl called Janet, from the North, who was also looking for a room, so we decided to share together. I gave my landlady a week's notice and moved to freedom.

Southwood Court was a vast building that had been divided into about fifteen bedsitting rooms. It had a crumbling elegance and was set in spacious grounds with a high brick wall surrounding it. The landlady was also vast and we, rather cruelly, nicknamed her "Elephant Bum" – not just because of her overall size, but when we spied her knickers on the washing line, the name fitted! Her husband was small and bespectacled and would lower his eyes when any nubile female students sunned themselves on the communal lawn. It was perfect for me. There was camaraderie, fun, gossip, discussion about the arts and I met my future husband in that urban arcadia.

Learning to act was hard work. When you go to the theatre to see a performance by a virtuoso, it looks so easy – but I had to learn the essential tools that contribute to the impression of ease. Lessons consisted of learning to breathe properly from the diaphragm and to project your voice so that you could be heard within the total confines of a large auditorium; learning to move gracefully, to dance, to fence and of course to act. One had to learn how to get into the head and heart of the person you were portraying, in order that the character became alive and believable to an audience. Wherever you were, on a train, a bus, the tube, in the pub, you learnt to observe people. Your next part could draw from the characteristics and movements of total strangers. After being denied contact with the general public for so many years, I was enthralled to discover such a diversity of characters. The college contained its own colourful personalities.

In my first month, I met two actors who would be significant throughout my life. James Villiers was a tall, aristocratic, good-looking young man who spoke with an upper class accent. He would look down at you with his sleepy, sexy eyes and drawl, "Don't be so common, luvvie." He was proud of his ancestry, which went back to the Duke of Buckingham, and although he was rich in comparison to me, and to most other students, he was as mean as buggery. We all caught on to this failing and would try to get him to buy a round in the pub – but his hand remained firmly in his pocket! James, or Jimmie as we called him, decided he had fallen in love with me. He asked me out to the cinema in Leicester Square to see the film *The Greatest Show on Earth*. He actually paid for my ticket! We held hands and saw the film through twice. Afterwards, in a tiny Bistro lit by candles stuck in Mateuse Rose bottles, he told me he loved me, but I was seeing another student then from the Guildhall School of Drama, called Peter. Peter's brother, Walla, was at the PARADA with Jimmie and me. I gently told Jimmie of my involvement with another. Next day Walla warned him to stay away from me otherwise he and his four brothers would ensure that Jimmie would never be able to find a job as a leading man, but would only be cast as an ex-boxer! Jimmie would recount how he went to see the same film for the third time, alone, which he could barely see through a mist of tears. We stayed friends for many years and a decade later he married one of my best friends and I was the matron of honour at their wedding.

The other character I became friendly with was Robin Ray, son of the then famous comedian Ted Ray, and the brother of Andrew Ray, a successful young actor. Robin did not want to be an actor – the piano was his great love – but his father insisted on him being in the "business". Robin was small and slim with piercing blue eyes and very intelligent, he was also a cinema buff. We would go to the cinema with packets of marmite sandwiches and a thermos of tea to watch any new film on the circuits. We munched our way through the performances, then, we would discuss every aspect of the film. Robin eventually became the compere of a cinema quiz programme on television. He was the foremost specialist on the cinema at that time. So, his father, Ted, was satisfied. Robin continued to play the piano in his spare time.

In my first term at PARADA a new girl joined my class half way through the term. She had one leg in a plaster cast and was extremely shy. I felt sorry for her because by then I knew most of the other students, so I went to sit beside her to engage her in conversation to help make her feel at ease. Julie was her name, she was blonde and blue-eyed and very pretty. She had broken her leg whilst skiing when she was at a finishing school in Switzerland. Gradually we became friends and she told me about her family. Her mother was the beautiful, intelligent, avant-garde writer and film director, Jill Craigie, who was a feminist and socialist. Jill had recently married the charismatic and eloquent labour MP Michael Foot and Julie was feeling resentful of her mothers' new relationship; she had just returned from boarding school and wanted all her mothers' attention. I knew how she felt.

"Will you be my cousin, Lizzie?" Julie pleaded, her large blue eyes filling with tears, "I feel so alone." At sixteen I became an adopted cousin to Julie and found a friendship that lasted throughout my life. Later I was accepted into her volatile family and Jill and Michael Foot became my mentors and helped to shape my attitudes and thoughts in my formative years.

There was another girl at college who Julie should have chosen as her cousin because they were virtual replicas of each other. Mary Selway was taller and more confident and glamorous, her beautiful eyes were heavily mascaraed and she always looked elegant compared to the rest of the scruffy students. Mary knew London well and with her air of sophistication and dry humour she was a welcome member of our newly found clique. Later she gave up the theatre to become one of the most formidable and well respected casting directors in the film business. Forty years later, she and Julie still looked so alike that when Sean Connery approached Mary at the Ivy restaurant with a, "Well, hello Julie." Mary realised why Sean had mistaken her for his ex-girlfriend!

I enjoyed the time spent in my leisure hours at Southwood Court as much as the time devoted to learning to act. The extra-curricular activities there surpassed any farce I was studying. Brian Charteris, who had introduced me to the mad house, was a wheeler-dealer character; he always had a car, usually an old one that was constantly breaking down and, although he was small and stocky, he managed to "pull" the girls because they were impressed he had transport. Most of us went by foot or bus or tube, where we tried to avoid paying fares.

I was caught on one occasion with no ticket and used my acting skills and tears to plead in court that my paltry grant of three pounds a week did not cover my fares to college. I was let off with a reprimand. No doubt my mini skirt and expanse of leg helped sway the male magistrate's decision. I was not a feminist in those days! Our biggest outlay, apart from the rent was the gas meter. During the cold winter evenings we would huddle around the toxic fire as it hungrily devoured our shillings' worth, then we knocked on somebody else's door to see if they had any warmth. Brian found a way to pick the lock on his gas meter and showed us how to put the same shilling through time and time again. We could cook, have numerous baths and avoid hypothermia!

One night there was a knock on the door and Brian peered in.

"Hi, Lizzie, are you dressed? I want you to meet my new roommate, Ronald Fraser, he's at RADA."

Brian was followed by a young man wearing a kilt. He had red hair, freckles, a broken nose and the smallest mouth I have ever seen, but his eyes were large and brown and expressive in his broad, open face. When he spoke, I was fascinated that such a beautiful voice could come out of that tiny aperture of a mouth. He immediately captured our attention and after brewing mugs of coffee, Ronnie asked us if we would like to hear his audition piece for the RADA. Janet, Brian and I settled on the metal beds and listened. It was a monologue from Shakespeare, I can't remember which one, but I do remember being transfixed by his delivery and personality. *He's going to be famous*, I thought. We quizzed him about life at RADA where we all hoped to end up.

Ronnie and Brian were like brothers to me. I now had an extended family, they protected me from unsuitable suitors (there were many of those), and laughter was paramount. Ronnie and I had the same sense of humour: self-deprecating and slapstick. Brian and Ronnie would creep into our room at night when Janet and I were asleep and cook themselves baked beans and toast – using my shilling because they had spent theirs – I would wake to the delicious smell and try to be angry but Ronnie always made me laugh instead. One day when I had an important rehearsal with Robin Ray, who was directing an Ibsen play with me in the title role, they tied me to my bed and locked me in my room. My tearful pleading and angry shouting was in vain. After an hour they opened the door. I did not think that was funny and refused to talk to them for a week. We were inseparable then. They even came down to Bournemouth to meet my parents and spent a happy, drunken Christmas at our house. We had to attend a formal dance and I remember trying to squeeze Ronnie into my grandfather's dinner suit. Grandpa was five foot nothing and Ronnie was much taller; his red tartan socks covered the lower leg and the whole ensemble looked ridiculous.

There were days out on the River Thames. A jovial, plump actor called Paddy Newell from a rich family had an ancient Rolls Royce. We would cram into it and drive down to Maidenhead singing and laughing. The Roller often broke down and Paddy would unscrew the Silver Lady from the bonnet and we would hitch hike for the remainder of the journey. They christened me "Dizzie Lizzie" because of my inability to add up and would mimic me adding up on my fingers. The name stuck for years – until I bought a calculator.

Why were summers always warmer in the old days? I remember hazy hot days when students would congregate on the lawn of Southwood Court to rehearse *A Midsummer Night's Dream*. We would loll under the trees with our scripts, lunches, drinks and chocolates around us while Oberon and Titania capered in the long grass. However, Mr Elephant Bum did not appreciate our rendering of the Bard and one warm day he appeared with his motorised lawnmower and chewed up our chocolates and scripts, scattering us in all directions.

Mrs Elephant Bum by then also had enough of her student lodgers. She discovered that there was no money in the gas meters! We were all given notice, but she knew Ronnie and Brian were the main culprits and she bundled all their possessions into plastic bags and drove immediately to RADA where she dumped them on the steps for the principal and all the passers-by to see. Ronnie went back to his ex-lodgings that night and wrote, "FUCK OFF, ELEPHANT BUM" in chalk on the wall surrounding Southwood Court. I still had a week to find digs and would slink in through the gates of the graffiti-defiled walls, praying no one would see that I lived there.

I moved to the antithesis of my previous digs and I went to stay with my new "cousin" Julie and her parents, Michael Foot and Jill Craigie. They lived in a huge house in Hampstead. Jill interviewed me before she let me have a room.

"Lizzie, I would like to have £3 a week for the rent. Is that OK with you?"

I was on a grant from Hampshire council of £10 a week – which was supposed to include everything: food, fares, and clothes. In Jill's home I had a carpeted room, a bathroom of my own and the use of their huge kitchen which felt like luxury!

"Yes Jill, I will pay you every week." I did struggle to find the amount, but I was so grateful and happy to be part of this fascinating, artistic, political and famous family that I would have starved rather than renege on my word.

Years later when I was applying for a job and asked Jill to give me a reference she wrote, "*Lizzie is a conscientious person: she paid her rent every week although she was a student with very little income and despite having to forego other luxuries*". Jill wrote my reference on a sheet of paper headed, "The House of Commons", but she had crossed out the heading and put her personal address! Michael Foot at that time was no longer a Member of Parliament.

Michael Foot in 1950 was the Labour Member of Parliament for Plymouth Devonport Constituency. Michael's parallel career was as an editor of *Tribune* and the *Evening Standard*. He was probably the greatest orator to have held the floor in Parliament for decades – but, above all, he was a humanitarian with a compelling character and sense of humour.

I knew nothing of politics when I first went to live with the family; in fact, I am ashamed to say that prior to my "enlightenment", I voted Conservative! That soon changed. During my stay with Michael and Jill, I met luminaries such as Aneurin Bevan and Neil Kinnock; other visitors to the house included writers, actors and film directors. I passed Gregory Peck on the stairs one day, and Spike Milligan was a great friend of Michael's. I was in awe of them, but they accepted me and teased me constantly, knowing I was studying to be a thespian. Peggy Ashcroft was a friend of Jill's. I could not believe my luck! The greatest actor of that era would say, "Hello," as I popped into the living room to say goodnight! The house in Hampstead was the centre of the literati and I was part of it.

In the mornings Michael would give me a lift to the RADA on his way to the House of Commons. He had an old Ford Prefect car that he parked on the hill opposite the house; we would then be assured of a rolling start, should the engine not spark into life. We didn't talk much, because his mind was on politics and the speeches he was to deliver in the House. Occasionally he would say, "Are you hungry, little tic?" (This was his affectionate term for Julie and me. Not a very attractive nickname, but when spoken by Michael it sounded endearing).

"Yes, a little," I would answer.

"Let's stop for a bite then."

We would then make a detour to Curzon Street to his favourite small restaurant and scoff sausages and baked beans and croissants. Michael always paid and I never needed to go to the canteen on those special days, saving several pounds of my meagre grant.

Jill lived in a perpetual state of anxiety concerning Michael's lack of thought about his clothing. He would wear odd socks and any old clothes that were at hand. Indeed his appearance did cause much criticism, when he was Labour Leader in 1981 (at the wreath-laying ceremony, at the Cenotaph on Remembrance Day). He wore what was called "a donkey jacket". Actually it was a type of duffel coat. Michael did not make it generally known that the Queen Mother had described it as a "sensible coat for a day like this". Well, it was, because Michael suffered from asthma and needed the warmth.

I was always short of money. Jill knew this and would help in every way that she could. She directed a TV documentary about a drama student coming to London, and I was made the subject. I portrayed this penniless student having to take different jobs to augment my grant. I worked as a waitress in the fashionable coffee shops of that era. One job was in Soho, where Tommy Steele was playing his guitar in the basement. I got the sack after falling down the cellar stairs with a loaded tray! I worked at the Ionic Cinema in Golders Green as an usherette. I saw *Moulin Rouge* fifty times, and discovered a dead old age pensioner still in his seat after a matinee, but I enjoyed being in the spotlight selling ice creams when the organ came up in the interval. I usually spent the extra money on clothes, knowing that I would soon need to look well dressed when I went for auditions.

I had plenty of boyfriends: Peter Gilmore was my first serious relationship. I fell in love with his singing voice before we became an item. Peter appeared in *Paint Your Wagon* in Bournemouth once (my parents were living there at the time). Peter was very short-sighted and without his glasses (there were no contact lenses in those days) he had difficulty in finding his exact place in the chorus line! However, he went on to become a big star after appearing in the television production of *The Onedin Line*.

I was still a virgin at nineteen until I met Anthony Newley. Julie was going out with Leslie Bricusse, a talented young songwriter and Leslie and Tony were collaborating on a new musical. Tony had been a child star when he played the Artful Dodger in a film of *Oliver Twist* in 1948. He was trying to make the transition from a child star to an adult actor. Tony was out of work when I met him, but he was charming, funny and very persuasive. I had done everything but the actual act of penetration; I can remember thinking as he took my virginity, *I hope this will make me a better actress!* because it was bloody painful and not really enjoyable.

Jill and Michael left their beautiful house in Hampstead to move to a smaller house in Maidavale, so I had to look for digs elsewhere. Back to linoleum on the floor, shillings in the meter and baths with an evil smelling geyser which ran out of hot water before the bath was full. I found a room off Baker Street above a dry cleaners, which was warm and nearer to the centre of London. I needed to be nearer to town because I would be leaving RADA soon; there I would be closer for auditions and hopefully the offer of my first acting job.

ON STAGE

ACT II

Actors need to have professional photographs taken to distribute to agents and possible contacts who might give one a job. I paid a lot of money for these. I was contacted by a reputable agent after I left RADA He had seen me at the end of term production. I thought he would offer me a job immediately. He didn't. Later on, when I was short of photographs, I went to see him to get my photos back. He had written on the back, "*Good leading lady material at forty*" I was then nineteen!

There is an agency in London for Actors called Spotlight. It has a huge book of photographs of most of the actors in England. My photo was in it. I got a call from Spotlight telling me that a producer in a good repertory would like to see me regarding casting in his new season in Chesterfield. Oh! The joy and the wonder, that someone was interested in me. I dressed in my best suit – I only had one – and raced up the stairs to the dingy office in Leicester Square. The producer, Gerald Glaister, was seated behind a desk. He shook my hand and then explained what he wanted for a season of weekly repertory in Chesterfield. He wanted a juvenile lead. His first play was to be *The Merchant of Venice*. He wanted me to play Nerissa, Portias' handmaiden. Then he said, "Can I see your legs?"

What for? I thought. In Shakespeare's day all the women wore long skirts, but I realised I would be playing modern day roles as well. I showed him my legs (they are very shapely) and he seemed impressed. I got the job, my first in the professional theatre. I ran downstairs crying with happiness and met Ronnie at the Arts Theatre Club. We drank Merrydown Cider and hugged and promised to stay in touch no matter where we were.

I took the train to Chesterfield, the town with the crooked spire, scared and yet happy. On arrival, I had been told where I could stay for the first night, a room in a boarding house near to the theatre. It was very basic, with a pot under the bed and no bath in sight. After dumping my luggage, I wandered out to find a cafe. Two young men were sitting inside a steamy fish and chip cafe nearby; they waved at me as I came in. They were also with the theatre company. One, blond and handsome, was David McAllum, employed as the assistant stage manager. The other, dark and gorgeous, was Ted Follows, the stage manager of the company. We talked and compared thoughts about our new surroundings and the future productions, then linked arms and wandered back to our digs. I lay on my iron bed thanking whoever was up there, above the crooked spire, for my first job in theatre.

The cast included the very talented Margaret Tyzak and Nigel Davenport. We would put on a new play every week, rehearsing in the morning and afternoon and learning our lines after the evening performance. Luckily I had a photographic memory, but I did not have large parts to learn there.

The first night of *The Merchant of Venice* was memorable for me. The smell of the size, the lights and the dust particles caught in the beams; the shared dressing room with sticks of make-up laid out in front of me; the voice over the Tannoy calling first, "Ten minutes, please" then, "five minutes, please"; the thrill of knowing you were going to be out there, on stage in front of a live audience and you would be creating a world of make believe for a paying audience!

I got the sack after three months. I started having an affair with a local farmer and we would be out every night until very late. I forgot my lines; I was told by the producer, Glaister, that I was not able to project my voice and couldn't be heard past the first six rows. I returned to London ashamed and repentant, determined never to let my love life interfere with my acting career again. After three months I found another job in a repertory company in Bangor, in Northern Ireland. The director and producer was a charismatic woman called Marjory Mason who told me that it was a limited season of six months at the New Theatre. I was to be the juvenile lead and she had planned many good plays. I was thrilled to be working again and as most of the males in the company were gay, I did not have a problem with being distracted from my work!

I was a terrible giggler on stage; if things go wrong during a performance in the business and you can't contain your laughter, it is called *corpsing*. In a comedy called, 'See How They Run', I had to pour milk from a jug onto my cereal. The milk was bad and came out in a large solid lump-plop into my bowl. I couldn't stop laughing until Marjory threw a spoon at me and kicked me under the table.

The theatre critic wrote in that weeks' paper: "Elizabeth Howe (my stage name) seems to have been enjoying the play as much as the audience!"

I was very happy during my time in Bangor. My acting skills, improved and so did my confidence. I could be heard at the back of the stalls, even though there were no microphones then, and I played a variety of challenging roles. I shared a flat with a member of the company, Pam, above a bakers' shop. We were woken in the early morning with the delicious smell of baking bread and our heating bills were not excessive. In my spare time I walked by the sea or went to the cinema, which was free to all actors in the repertory company. I learnt my lines every night to perfection.

Then I met an Irishman called Holmes. He would come to the theatre every week and wait at the stage door for me to appear. He asked me out on a Sunday. We drove over the border to Eire and I discovered Dublin and the Southern Ireland. It was very different from the North and the people were wild and unpredictable. Holmes was a heavy drinker, I suppose in retrospect he might have been an alcoholic, but he was fun and rich and he had a Jaguar which he let me drive down the Irish lanes, despite the fact that I did not have a licence! He took me to Belfast to see Ronnie who was appearing with the Old Vic on tour at the time. They got on so well, I felt excluded. They had drinking in common. I returned to England when my contract had finished and I did not see Holmes again, but I have to thank him for my discovery of the magic of Southern Ireland.

Carl Clopet, a manager and horse racing fanatic, employed me as the juvenile lead for his next summer season in Cork. I packed my many trunks – in those days an actor had to take a lot of clothes for the various roles they had to play in, except for period costume, which was hired. I caught the ferry from Fishguard, sharing a cabin with four nuns who were sick all the way. Luckily I was on the top bunk. Arriving in Cork, I got a taxi. I had been given an address of digs near to the theatre and as the taxi man unloaded my trunks, half of the inhabitants of the street turned out to look.

"What a fine lady she must be with so much luggage."

"So why is she staying here and not in the hotel?"

I smiled, tipped the taxi man and knocked on the door of the digs. It was opened by a stout, buxom woman with a cat in her arms.

"Would you be my paying guest then?"

"Yes, I am Elizabeth Howe."

"Welcome and come into our happy home."

It was a happy home, despite the fact that the bathroom had a lavatory cistern sticking out of the floor and the loo was outside in a shed. Maria and Sean were brother and sister. Sean did not seem to work, but once a month he would disappear for two days. I thought he was involved with the IRA and possibly a gunrunner.

They were warm and friendly and breakfast was a feast. They would include the cat at the table and put glasses on its nose so it could see the menu! However, I got fed up with having to go outside to pee in the middle of the night and having to climb a ladder out of the kitchen to do my ablution, so I found a more modern flat which I shared with Pauline who was the assistant stage manager in the company.

The Cork Opera House was a magnificent building. It was built originally in 1877 and many famous opera singers and companies had performed there. The auditorium seated 1,000 people; there was a circle and the "Gods", or the "jam shelf", as the top seating was known. I really needed to project my voice in that vast space.

Carl Clopet, the manager and sometime producer, was a genial man who we liked, because he would give us all Thursday afternoons off so that he could go to the races. He had female twins who always worked with him. One, Prudence, was the secretary and accountant; the other, Priscilla, was the leading lady and, we suspected, his mistress. Priscilla must have been about forty-five but she played every leading role! I was meant to be the juvenile lead but got very few of those parts.

Cork audiences are renowned for being the hardest to please. There was a classic example when we were playing *Dracula*. Priscilla, as usual, had the female lead. It was a Saturday night and the theatre was packed. John Cater had to deliver these lines to her:

"I pray to God I may never see your face again."

An Irish voice from the gallery shouted out:

"And by Gorrah we've seen it enough as it is."

Then the whole of the gallery started rolling their Guinness bottles down the steps, preventing any further dialogue on stage.

1955 was one of the hottest summers ever recorded in Ireland. Cork was near the sea and after the shows we would go for moonlight swims to a small bay nearby. I got to know two brothers, Jonny and Humphrey, who owned a pub called the Hay Loft. We would stop off there after hours and drink and watch Humphrey do his headstand on the bar, balancing a pint glass on his feet. One night there was a loud knock on the door after twelve, midnight. Jonny opened it to discover a policeman (or Guardia) standing there. He sauntered in and got out his notebook and pencil. I was sitting at the bar with a Guinness in my hand.

"Now, young lady, what might your name be?"

It flashed through my mind that if I was caught drinking out of hours, it would be really bad publicity for the theatre, so I mumbled, "Elizabeth Howgego." This was my real name, but not the one I was billed as in the theatre.

"What? Ach, it's too difficult to write down. Give me a pint, please, Jonny."

There was one play in which I was allowed to play the juvenile lead: I was a rebellious, sullen teenager in the comedy called, *My Wife's Lodger*. Priscilla could not shed enough years to play that part! Dandy Nicholls and Leo Franklin were guest actors who played my parents. The play was a huge success and, after the season closed, Dandy asked if I would like to come on tour in England with the play. Of course I said, "Yes." I loved Ireland and the crazy people but I knew I had to return to England if I wanted to be seen in the theatre and to be discovered! The beautiful Cork Opera House burnt down just after I left. The reason was faulty wiring. It was rebuilt in 1963 and continues to be a centre for artistic excellence.

The Theatre Royal in Brighton was our first booking in England. I was getting nearer to London and many friends came down to see the play. I had telegrams and flowers and my parents travelled from Bournemouth to see me in the show. They were bursting with pride and my mother kept turning to strangers, saying, "That's my daughter up there on stage." Then we played at Hastings. I had my twenty-first birthday there; I was having an affair with the stage manager at that time. Ben made the day very special for me with presents of jewellery and flowers and the cast threw a party for me backstage after the show. As I blew out the candles, I felt inordinately proud of myself. I was working in the theatre, whilst many students in my class at RADA had never set foot on the boards after leaving. I was doing what I enjoyed most in life and earning a living from it.

My ambition was to go to London to find a job, either as an understudy or at least in a fortnightly repertory near to the heart of the theatre. Then, agents could come and see me and recognise my talent. I was lucky. I found a job in the chorus in a respected fortnightly repertory theatre in Hornchurch. They were putting on a pantomime, *Little Red Riding Hood*, for a three-week season. The chorus consisted mostly of Ballet Rambert students. I had studied ballet at RADA, but I also had a very high instep (hereditary) and, whilst the Rambert students had to practice for years to develop their points, I was a natural. So I did not have to wear those agonising block point ballet shoes, and glided around on semi points, which were not so tiring.

It was a fantastic season. The talented cast included, Bernard Cribbins, David Dodimead, Patsy Byrne, and Elvi Hale. The producer, Stuart Burge, created Christmas magic for the children, who shouted at the villain and were spellbound by the fantasy they witnessed on stage. I stayed with my sister, who fortunately lived in Hornchurch at the time. We had Christmas at her place with my parents and my little niece, Debbie. After the pantomime, Stuart asked me to stay on in the company. I agreed. I played opposite many good actors and appeared in some classical plays, developing my acting skills. I enjoyed meeting new members of the company. I am convinced that actors call everybody "darling" because in their work they meet so many people, they can't possibly remember all the names.

During my years in repertory I always kept in touch with Ronnie, either by letter or by phone if we had one (there were no mobiles in those days). He was playing in Coventry Rep and would come down to London on a Sunday. We would meet up and go for drinks at the Arts Club or the Salisbury Pub, an actor's favourite drinking den in St Martins Lane. He had sent me a very affectionate letter on my birthday, which surprised me. We had a close relationship and enjoyed each other's company, but that was it. Then one fateful night we went to a friend's party. We went to bed together and made love. He was no longer my brother. In the morning I was confused and upset. Why had I allowed myself to sleep with him? It changed our relationship. I loved him, but I was not in love with him. Ronnie was embarrassed too. He had to catch the train back to Coventry and asked if I would come up and stay with him when my work had finished. I replied vaguely and promised to be in touch. I needed time to think about my feelings.

I did go to Coventry. Ronnie said he was in love with me. I thought I was with him as well. Three weeks later he proposed. I did not accept then, I needed time to think. What would life be like with this talented, sociable, irascible, heavy drinking funny man? Neither of us had an offer of jobs in the future. We had nowhere to live and little money. I asked friends what I should do. Nearly all of his male friends said Ronnie would not change, I would have to put up with his drinking and his late nights, but, he would be a star, and he loved me. Wasn't that enough? I said yes to him.

When I told my mother that Ronnie and I wanted to get married she burst into tears! She had known him for years and he teased her and made her laugh, but I presume she wanted someone better for her daughter, not an unpredictable penniless actor. She brushed away her tears, hugged me and said, "I just hope you will be happy."

I was, for seven years.

RONNIE - THE FATHER

ACT III

Ronald Gordon Fraser, my husband, was born on 11th of April 1930 in Ashton-under-Lyne in Lancashire. His mother told me that when he arrived his head was covered with a caul; this, according to his mother, Annie, was a good omen. I cannot deny that his earlier life was governed by great strokes of luck, combined with a prodigious talent.

Ronnie's father, William Fraser, was a Scotsman. He was a decorator and house painter by profession. His mother, Annie Porteous, was from Bonnybridge in Scotland. She worked for the Singer Sewing Machine Company and in 1905 her right arm was amputated below the elbow by machinery in the factory. Annie was a tall handsome woman and her disability obviously did not deter William, who proposed marriage to her in Clydebank; they then went to live in Ashton-under-Lyne where it was easier to find work. Ronnie's father was disappointed that his son was not "born in Scotland".

"It was the only mistake your mother made, that you were born abroad," he told young Ronnie, "but, there was no doubt about your nationality, the tartan shone out of your eyes."

I am not clear about some of Ronnie's early life, he did not find it easy to talk about the fact that his father died when he was young and that his mother married again. His stepfather was a disciplinarian and there was tension between them. Ronnie was forbidden to play the piano, which was a source of joy for him. He therefore spent a lot of time outside the house with school friends and became interested in amateur dramatics. Perhaps he decided to live in a fantasy world rather than to acknowledge the reality of his daily strictures.

The house where he spent most of his formative years was a terraced Victorian cottage. The front door opened directly into the sitting room, which was dominated by a large cast iron fireplace and provided warmth against the harsh Lancashire days and nights. There was always a kettle hanging over the coals to provide hot water for washing and endless cups of tea. The lavatory was outside in a shed; upstairs there were two small bedrooms. Leading up to the bedrooms was a flight of very steep stairs, precipitous is the correct word. Ronnie, at aged one, tumbled from top to bottom, resulting in the first break to his nose. Later he fell out of his pram and landed on his nose again. It must have been extremely difficult for his mother with her disability to cope with a growing toddler, but he survived.

Ronnie's face became his fortune! I have a photo of him sitting naked on a bearskin rug aged one. On top of the infant's chubby body is the unmistakable face of Basil Allenby Johnson or "Badger", who he played in *The Misfit*, a television series in 1970. He became one of the most sought-after character actors in show business, but as a young man he did not have the looks to attract the ladies – so, he developed charm, humour and a lovable personality, which was what attracted me to him from the beginning of our friendship.

On leaving school, Ronnie had to do his stint in the National Service. He joined the Seaforth Highlanders in North Africa then later on was posted to Cyprus. It was during this time that he was asked to replace a disc jockey and to play a few records. *What a lovely way to earn money*, he thought. On his discharge from the army, he auditioned for the Royal Academy of Dramatic Art and was accepted. Ronnie was given a scholarship and after two years studying and discovering the delights of the many London pubs, he was awarded the silver medal for his performance at the student matinee at RADA. Peter Crouch, a theatrical agent, saw him on stage and recognised Ronnie's exceptional talent and put him under contract. Peter became a great friend as well as an agent, also a generous provider of funds when jobs were not forthcoming!

Ronnie's first professional job was as a dresser to Sir Donald Wolfit. He also played a few small parts and helped, generally, behind the scenes. One night after the show, as Ronnie was removing his make-up, Wolfit remarked, "Fraser, I knew there was an *artist* on the wind machine tonight!"

In 1953 he understudied Noel Coward in *The Apple Cart* at the Haymarket theatre. He learnt that even the "Master", as Coward was known, was unsure of himself. Before his first entrance he would be shaking in the wings, but once on stage he was in command. Then came a season at the famous Glasgow Citizens Theatre where he played mostly character parts. A theatre critic wrote this of him:

"Ronald Fraser, the agreeable young man, whose nose always suggests he has just had a collision with a tram, is due to join the Old Vic Company..."

He did, from 1954 to 1955. The Old Vic Company was in the famous old theatre at Waterloo. There were many prestigious actors in the company: Paul Rogers, Eric Porter and John Neville. I had a ridiculous crush on John (he was married with children), and whenever I was in London I would go back stage to see Ronnie, but it was John I really wanted to see. Actors said John and I looked like brother and sister; that was the last thing I wanted to be!

After, The Old Vic Company went on tour to Ireland (where I caught up with Ronnie). He then joined the Midland Theatre Company in Coventry. He was clever enough to know that he could be branded as a Shakespearean actor if he did not try modern plays. Frank Dunlop was the inspired producer and there were a variety of plays and challenging roles for Ronnie to learn from; also, Coventry was only a train ride from London where I was living. After accepting Ronnie's proposal I would journey to Coventry on a Sunday; he had squalid digs, but that didn't matter, we were in love! We planned our marriage for next year when his contract had finished. It had to be in London because that was where most of our friends lived. Neither of us thought about money or a home – we just wanted to be together.

MR AND MRS

ACT IV

Our wedding was arranged by my parents. It was to be held at Church Row in Hampstead. They also made plans for the reception at Hampstead's 250 year old Burgh House. Most of the people they invited were unknown to me; they were old friends of theirs from India. I had chosen Julie and another close friend, Joan, to be my bridesmaids. Ronnie had insisted that the ushers, Sean Connery, James Copeland, Ian MacNaughton and David Butler wear kilts. They were all actors from Scotland. Ronnie would wear his Fraser tartan kilt. Brian Charteris, his best man, wore a hired dress suit. As I joined Ronnie at the altar, I was overpowered by the smell of alcohol. I remember thinking – "Is it easy to get a divorce!" The reception was a disaster. The actors Ronnie had invited on his stag night the evening before, turned up in droves. They were not allowed inside because the ancient floor would have collapsed. I spent my time inside smiling politely at my parents' friends or rushing outside to the balcony to laugh with my actor mates.

We did not have a honeymoon then. Ronnie was understudying Peter Ustinov in *Romanoff and Juliet*. When he finished his contract in that play we were both out of work. However, Ronnie, with his flair for making friends with the right people, had found a couple of theatrical managers who were putting on a season of repertory in St John's, Newfoundland. I was to be a stage manager and bit actress and Ronnie was to be the character actor.

"Where the fuck is Newfoundland?" I asked when he told me of the offer.

"It's near Canada," Ronnie replied, "I believe it's a bit cold, but it's work and Oliver and Leslie are great people."

We left from Liverpool on a rather old passenger ship. It turned out that we had been given separate cabins because we were on the passenger list under our stage names, Ronald Fraser and Elizabeth Howe. We made love as we were leaving Liverpool in our empty cabin. Everyone else was waving fond farewells to their loved ones. It was a long and rough trip. The leading lady, Moira (who I shared a cabin with) was seasick even before we left the dock. We played deck quoits in the swell of the Atlantic, cards through the day and night and at one stage there was only Ronnie and I and the crew left eating at the captain's table.

Newfoundland is a barren, generally cold island off the coast of Nova Scotia. The boat edged its way into the harbour between huge icebergs: magnificent, sculpted blocks of ice. This was our vista for three months. We would go to the theatre on a toboggan down the steep hill leading to St Johns, and after the performance or rehearsal, we climbed through the ice and snow to our digs, exhausted, but invigorated.

Oliver Gordon and Leslie Yeo, the managers, were determined to provide good entertainment to the population in this inhospitable region. The plays were varied and interesting. One production was *Rain*. Our leading lady, Moira, had long, tinted red hair; I knew this because we shared a bathroom and the sink had smears of red dye after she had been in there! She had an entrance to make in the play, but she caught her hair on a nail on one of the pieces of scenery and could not untangle herself. The actors on stage ad-libbed for some time, until the stage manager found a pair of scissors and cut off the entwined lock of hair. Moira was grateful, but furious that her tresses had been shortened.

Ronnie and I also worked for the Canadian Broadcasting Company recording plays when we were not rehearsing. We made a lot more money than we were paid at the theatre and managed to save it. It was the worst winter on record that year; we were meant to be going on to tour Canada after the season in Newfoundland, but the audiences dwindled as they just could not get to the theatre and we had to close. We met some wonderful people on the island, an English family who had settled there (God knows why), and had a memorable, snowy Christmas in their cosy home. We also entertained a thousand Mounties at their camp in the freezing wilderness of Newfoundland. We produced a review and in one of the sketches Ronnie did an act as an incompetent Conjurer, Tommy Cooper style. I was his assistant and had to appear in a top hat, a short red jacket, fishnet tights and high heels. There were whistles and shouts from the Mounties and a roar of applause. Afterwards Ronnie said, "I did not realise you were so sexy!" I didn't either.

We returned to England and were more than happy to be back in a reasonable climate again. We found a small flat in Maidavale, which we could now easily afford as we had our small savings from our work in Newfoundland. We both looked for jobs rather half heartedly, but decided to enjoy our leisure time. It was a glorious summer; we played tennis in the recreation ground opposite with baggy old racquets – the ball would actually get stuck in the strings. Julie, my friend and adopted cousin, was going out with Sean Connery and we would pile into her MG sports car and hurtle down to Leatherhead where Michael and Jill had been lent a small cottage on Beaverbrook's estate. The building was in the middle of a huge field and we had to dodge the cows and sometimes a bull to get to it. We swam in the pool at the bottom of Box Hill, walked in the woods, played Scrabble and chess and forgot about work for that idyllic summer.

Jill, Julie's mother, was not very happy about Julie's relationship with Sean. She spoke to Julie one day about her concern:

"Listen, darling," she said, "I know he is very good looking and all that, but he hasn't done much in the theatre or films, and I don't think he is going to become a star!"

Jill was wrong. Sean went on to become the best James Bond ever portrayed on screen and has produced some fine performances in many other films. Sadly for Julie their relationship finished when Sean met Diane Cilento and fell for her, and then subsequently married her.

Our savings ran out that summer therefore it became imperative to find a job. Ronnie did a few television plays and then was offered a contract with The Old Vic Company for the 1957–1958 season.

The Arts Council funded the company at the theatre in the Waterloo road. The brilliant director was Michael Benthall, and the cast included John Neville, Coral Browne, Barbara Jefford, Paul Daneman, Judi Dench and Robert Helpman. There were many other talented actors in the large company, and Ronnie was one of them.

The season opened with *Hamlet*; John Neville in the title role and Judi Dench as Ophelia. The first night critic mentioned Ronnie, although he only had a minor part in the play:

"Ronald Fraser gives another of his brilliant studies in character grotesque."

The Christmas show was *A Midsummer Night's Dream*. Frankie Howard was cast as Bottom. It was a brilliant and unexpected piece of casting but Michael Benthall knew Frankie would draw the crowds to The Old Vic. Ronnie was Flute and he told me about the tricks they would play on Frankie on stage. Frankie wore a toupee and was sensitive about his lack of hair. In one scene the artisans formed a circle around Bottom, in a dance, and they would try and dislodge his toupee with their arms. Frankie took it with good humour, but stuck his wig down more firmly during the rest of the run.

I was working at Keith Prowse ticket agency at that time and would go and meet Ronnie backstage after the show. One night Robert Helpman came into Ronnie's dressing room.

"Quick, come into my dressing room and see what I've got!"

We went to his room, after Ronnie had removed his make-up, knocked on the door and entered. In a chair was sitting a very large person with a blonde wig, a mink fur coat, lots of slap and with huge hands.

"This is Roberta Cowell," Robert said. "She saw the show tonight."

Roberta's deep voice replied, "Yes, and I loved it."

Helpman was staring at Roberta rudely, fascinated by her appearance. After the tall person had left the room, with extremely strong handshakes all round, Robert whispered, "Do you know who that was?"

"No," I replied.

"Let me tell you then. He used to be a man called Robert Cowell and was a racing driver, but he always felt that he was really a woman, so he had the operation! Poor darling, what a disaster. Any thoughts I had of changing my sex have been forgotten."

Helpman was gay and living with Michael Benthall at that time.

Sex change operations were very basic and painful in those days, with no hormones to gently adapt the body to the new gender; they were usually carried out in North Africa and not in hygienic surroundings. After Roberta's courageous transformation other transgender people dared to try an operation. April Ashley attracted a lot of publicity when she married an aristocrat. We met her in Marbella, as a tall beautiful redhead. Her operation had been more successful, but the hands were a give-away. Her marriage did not last long. This led to a lot of lewd conjecture in theatrical circles as to why it had failed!

FAME

ACT V

It was in 1959 that Ronnie first made a big impression in the theatre and film world. He had been gathering complimentary reviews in all the plays and television shows he had appeared in. I was thrilled for him. It was clear that my career was secondary to his. I appeared in pantomime in Salisbury as the Princess in *Alladin* for a Christmas season and then found jobs in London in commercials and at a telephone answering service, which employed actors who had to pretend to be in the home of the owner. It was money that we always needed, as theatrical salaries were not high (television paid better), but we never knew when we would be offered the next job.

The TV play, *The Pot Carriers*, written by Mike Watts, was the showcase that brought Ronnie to the attention of more directors and film producers. The play was about a group of "lags" in prison. Ronnie played a cheery, ingenious inmate who was always on the fiddle. He received excellent reviews for his performance and stole the show from Davy Kaye, his prisonmate.

Lindsay Anderson was casting a new play at The Royal Court Theatre. The play was *The Long and the Short and the Tall*, written by Willis Hall. Lindsay had seen Ronnie in *The Pot Carriers*, and asked him to join the cast of the new play. The main theme of the drama was about a lost patrol surrounded by the Japanese enemy in the Malayan jungle. Ronnie played Macleish, a Scottish corporal with a heart of gold. The main character, Private Bamforth was played by Peter O'Toole. The others in the strong cast were Robert Shaw, Edward Judd, David Andrews, Bryan Pringle, Alfred Lynch and Kenji Takaki, who was probably the only actor in a play who never spoke a word!

The Long and the Short and the Tall got rave reviews. We went to the mobile canteen on Waterloo Bridge, which was open all night, and waited for the papers to come out. When we read them we shouted and danced and hugged each other. All the critics were unanimous with their praise. Harold Hobson in his review spent half of the article praising Kenji Takaki (the Japanese actor) for his rendering of a silent prisoner, but Peter O'Toole became a star over night. Peter's understudy was Michael Caine, who took a longer time to reach stardom. Ronnie had favourable notices in all the papers and it seemed that the play was set for a long run.

The success of the play came at an opportune time in our lives, because I was pregnant.

Knowing that we had the security of a weekly salary, we decided to move.

We needed more rooms with a baby coming in August and found a maisonette in the Kilburn High Road. It was above a dress shop owned by the Mitchell Singers. This was ideal, because there was no one living below to complain about a crying baby, nor the stream of actors who would arrive late at night after the theatre.

We bought the necessary second-hand furniture and friends gave us their surplus items. Eclectic was the theme! We had three bedrooms, a kitchen, bathroom and living room overlooking the busy High Road, but for me the bonus was a tiny balcony at the back, which overlooked an overgrown garden that had a ladder for access.

In a long-running play the cast obviously spend many hours together, luckily they all got on well and we would spend time after the show in pubs and actors' clubs, relaxing and drinking. One night after a heavy session at the Salisbury pub in St Martin's Lane, Peter O'Toole, Ronnie, Robert Shaw, Bryan Pringle and I climbed into our tiny Austin Seven; O'Toole was driving and set off up St Martin's Lane the wrong way. It was a one-way street. Heavily pregnant I yelled, "Let me out, you maniac!"

"Let's play dodgems tonight," drunken Peter laughed as he narrowly missed a bollard and some pedestrians.

Ronnie, realising my distress (and not being as drunk as the others) managed to get Peter to stop the car. I fell out onto the pavement as a policeman strolled by.

"Are they giving you a problem, lady?" he asked.

"No, no," I replied. I was terrified that they would be charged with drinking and driving (there were no breathalysers in those days).

"I was feeling sick. Pregnant, you know," I patted my bulging stomach.

"Ah, yes," he nodded, "better to be in the fresh air."

I never again got in a car when Peter was driving. The tales of his erratic driving have become legendary!

On the 8th April 1959, *The Long and the Short and the Tall* transferred to the New Theatre in St Martin's Lane with the same cast. Ronnie had become very close to Peter and they remained friends for the rest of their eventful lives. Fred Zinnerman, the brilliant film director, had seen the play and was impressed with Ronnie's performance, we did not realise then how significant this was. Peter was later to be cast as Lawrence of Arabia after Hollywood producers had seen his outstanding portrayal of Bamforth.

I was working at Air France in the market research department, in Bond Street. There was a heat wave that summer and I remember lying down on the floor in the office at lunch to rest my huge stomach. I was booked into Queen Charlotte's Maternity Hospital for the delivery, recommended by our clever and sociable Irish doctor, Gerry Slattery, who was doctor to many theatrical personalities. My waters broke in the office and I was rushed to hospital. I was in labour for twenty four agonising hours; the doctors realised that it was not a straightforward delivery and I was given an anaesthetic. The baby was a girl; we named her Fiona, only because it was a Scottish name. When I first saw her, I wanted to give her back! It had been a "face presentation", in other words she came out face first, rather than the back of her head first. She had bruises all over her face and looked like a small boxer! The bruises went and I felt an overwhelming love for this miracle, this tiny soul, my first child.

Ronnie was a proud father and showed Fiona off to all his friends He had opened in a new play in the West End after the *Long and the Short and the Tall* closed. The play was *The Ginger Man* by J.P. Donleavey. Ronnie again received good reviews for his portrayal of a sex-hungry American student and friend of the lead character, Dangerfield, played by Richard Harris. Richard was a wild Irishman and a huge new talent to the theatrical scene. He had married an upper class girl, Elizabeth (much to her parents' dismay). They had two boys and we would meet together for meals and of course drinks, cementing the friendship between Ronnie and Richard. They became known as "The Hellraisers", along with other heavy drinkers such as O'Toole, Oliver Reed and Richard Burton. They were talented, famous, and had money to live life to the full – but always with a drink to support them.

Fred Zinnerman offered Ronnie a part in a film to be made in Australia, it was called, *The Sundowers*. The cast included famous international stars: the maverick Robert Mitchum was to play the lead, and Deborah Kerr, Peter Ustinov and Glynis Johns were other big names in the film. This offer was a huge chance for Ronnie to be known internationally and in November he left for Australia.

Fiona was only four months old and my days were filled with caring for a demanding baby. I received many affectionate letters from Ronnie telling me about the shooting of the film. He described the locations in the outback with derision: the heat was intense and he had to learn to shear sheep, which he found painful and cruel. Bob Mitchum and Ronnie became friends and they would go fishing together if they had any spare time. In the towns, Bob did not dare come out of his hotel because he would be surrounded by fans; he rectified this by living on a boat. Most days he would swim to work!

The location filming was due to finish at the end of December and earlier Ronnie had written to tell me he hoped to be home by Christmas. I did not hear from him for weeks (there was no internet nor emails in those days). Then a telegram arrived telling me when his plane was expected. Happy and excited to see my husband again, I dressed Fiona in her best clothes and I wore a new attractive outfit for our meeting at Heathrow Airport. Ronnie came through the doors looking tanned, with a beard and huge bags under his eyes that were a nasty shade of red. After many hugs and kisses and remarks about how Fiona had grown we drove back to Kilburn.

In the car I asked Ronnie why I had not heard from him for so long and why he was looking like an old tramp.

"Well, it's like this," he mumbled, "Mitchum asked me to go with him to Thailand after the shoot. Of course I said yes, we had a ghastly time in Australia and needed a holiday."

Ronnie then recounted some lurid tales about visiting bars in Thailand where the girls could draw pictures with a pen stuck up their fannies! I withdrew his arm from my shoulders and moved away. I tried to be magnanimous and accept that he and Bob needed this diversion after a gruelling time in Australia.

The rest of the film was to be shot in Pinewood Studios. Bob was staying at The Dorchester Hotel in Park Lane. One evening Ronnie rang.

"Lizzie, put on your best dress tonight, Mitchum has asked us over to his hotel for drinks."

This was the first time I would have the opportunity to meet this infamous star. I dressed with care in my little black cocktail dress and fishnet tights with sparkling diamante earrings, threw a white feather boa around my shoulders, and then hailed a taxi. Ronnie met me at The Dorchester.

"You look gorgeous, darling; come on, up we go."

We got out of the lift on the sixth floor and rang the bell to Bob's suite. Minutes later the door opened and Bob stood there stark naked except for a tie loosely slung round his neck! I tried to avert my eyes from his extremely large penis and to focus on his battered, but attractive face. He ushered us into the bedroom and asked us what we were drinking, then went to the kitchen to prepare our orders.

I noticed that there was a female form covered by a sheet lying on the bed. I knew it was a woman because of the painted toenails protruding from the sheet. Bob returned with our drinks and continued talking. He paid no attention to the form on the bed; he was witty and a delightful conversationalist. After an hour the body started to move slightly and I nudged Ronnie.

"Shall we go into the kitchen and get some more drinks?"

Ronnie understood the need to leave the bedroom and we collapsed into giggles as we refreshed our glasses. After a short while we re-entered the bedroom to find a middle aged blonde woman, dressed in cashmere and pearls, standing by the bed; she extended her hand to greet us.

"So nice to meet you both," Bob ushered her to the door and virtually pushed her outside.

"Who was that?" Ronnie asked.

"I don't know," Bob replied. "Some neighbour from down the corridor."

The Associated British Picture Corporation had offered Ronnie a film contract, with the stipulation that he made one film a year for seven years. He had been compared to Humphrey Bogart and Victor McLaglen because of his rugged face and his versatile acting ability. Peter Crouch, his agent advised Ronnie to accept.

Then followed continuous work and the filming of *The Long and the Short and the Tall* at Elstree Studios. The lead was played by Laurence Harvey, as O'Toole was now filming *Lawrence of Arabia*. Richard Harris joined the cast and so did my old friend David McCallum. The film did not get good reviews, but before the first night, Ronnie had to leave England to go to South Africa where he was contracted to appear in a film called *The Hellions*.

I received many descriptive and loving letters from Ronnie whilst he was filming in Pretoria. He disliked the racial attitudes to black people and the locations were miles from civilisation, meaning no drink could be found! In March I realised that I was pregnant again and wrote to tell him that the new baby would arrive in October.

He had been cast in a new film in Israel starting on the 22nd April 1961. This meant we would not see each other for six months because he would fly directly from South Africa to Israel. In his next letter he wrote:

"You are to come out to Israel with Fiona to join me. I will pay for you to fly first class. No arguing, Lizzie. Peter Crouch will make all the arrangements. I love you both."

I also loved Ronnie's spontaneity and generosity and was thrilled to be embarking on this adventure, even if I had a naughty toddler to care for and was pregnant again.

The film was titled *The Best of Enemies*. It was an American-Italian production by Dino de Laurentiis and was directed by Guy Hamilton. The story was meant to take place in Ethiopia during World War II, and presented the dilemma of an Italian captain who wanted to release his British prisoners of war so that the British Army would leave his corps alone. The tribal African warriors sabotaged the escape plans, removing all the soldiers' shoes and forcing both nationalities to become "friends" in order to survive the trek through the desert. David Niven played the commanding British major and Alberto Sordi was the flamboyant Italian captain.

I was met at Tel Aviv airport by my emotional and loving husband. Noel Harrison, also in the cast, was with him and we drove in the dark to the first location – Bershaver. What a dump! It was a tiny town and camel market and it was here that all the best camels were brought to be sold. These amazing animals, known as, "the ships of the desert" would be paraded through the streets, blinking their beautiful eyelashes and spitting and biting anyone they did not like.

Luckily the cast and crew were moved after a few days to a nicer location. We stayed in Eilat, right on the Red Sea. Ronnie would leave early in the morning to film in the surrounding desert and I would take Fiona down to the sea to swim and play in the hot sand. The heat was intense, reaching forty degrees centigrade and there was a hot dry wind always blowing from the desert. I foolishly kept Fiona to her old routine and we would be the only ones out in the mid-day sun, until I became ill. The doctor told me I must take salt pills and *not* go out with Fiona after noon. The cast of the film also took salt pills before they went to work.

There were several other wives and girl friends of the cast and crew on location in Eilat. I became friendly with David Nivens' second wife, Yordis. She was a tall, beautiful redhead who adored Fiona and would keep her amused when I was tired. Yordis could not have children, but later on they adopted two children and named one girl Fiona. Also, I spent time with the girlfriend of one of the Italian cameramen. Lucia was very critical of my swimming costume; it was a floral tent, made to cover my large stomach and very un-sexy!

"You cannota wear thata," she insisted. "Looka here, I give you my bikini."

So I wore it. I showed off my bump and swam freely without the weight of my "tent" which filled with water and dragged me down.

The beach and the Red Sea was the hub of our social gatherings. After the insufferable heat of working all day in the desert, everyone would swim and relax. Niven sauntered to the shore with a towel draped over his shoulders; in contrast, Sordi would arrive with a retinue of followers carrying his towel, hat, sun cream and chair. Niven could not always relax because some of the locals would come to the beach to stare at the great actor.

"Are you David Niven?" they asked.

"Certainly not. Who is he?" Niven replied. David was the most charming and unspoilt star I had ever met.

One day we were assembled on the beach and Ronnie was gazing at the outline of Jordan, to the east of Eilat.

"You know, my mate Peter O'Toole is over there filming *Lawrence*," he remarked. "Pity we can't go and see him."

The rules in those days forbad any border crossings. Two burly extras heard this remark.

"You want a bet, mate?"

"What do you mean?"

"We will go and see him if you like – for a bet, but you've got to make it worth our while."

"O.K. you're on, but you will have to take a note from me and bring one back from Peter, to prove you have seen him," Ronnie laughed.

"Go and write the note then and seal it in a waterproof container," the Australian extra replied.

Everyone was mystified as to how the extras would get to the tents we could see in the distance, without being arrested. They set off on lilos in the dark, paddling with their arms across the large expanse of the Red Sea to where the tents were pitched on the Jordanian shore. They made it there and found Peter, delivered the wet note from Ronnie and waited for the reply, but they could not move their arms to paddle back; they were hidden in a tent until they had recovered. Then paddled back a day later to claim their bet!

The location work was finished and the rest of the film was due to be completed in the studios in Rome. Ronnie had to fly back to England first, because he had a voiceover to do for *The Hellions*. Yordis asked me if I would like to go to Switzerland with her to the house she and David lived in. We were all exhausted from the heat and I was feeling weak and sick, but I knew Ronnie would be joining us in Rome later, so I declined her kind offer. How I wish I had accepted.

Fiona and I went to stay in a five-star hotel near the Villa Borghese Gardens. I would push her around the beautiful grounds and let her toddle unsteadily on the grass. I was happy to be in a more temperate climate. One morning, I was having breakfast in the hotel dining room, when I suddenly felt an unusual pain in my womb; it felt as though the baby was dropping. I was four months pregnant. I knew I had to lie down, but I had Fiona with me. An aristocratic elderly gentleman was sitting near me, quietly enjoying a coffee behind his newspaper.

"Please, sir," I shouted. "I need your help now."

"What, me?"

"Yes, you! I think I am about to have a miscarriage and I need you to look after my little daughter. Put her in the pram and take her for a walk. Her name is Fiona."

He jumped to his feet and carefully placed Fiona in her pushchair and walked to the door.

"Say bye-bye to Mummy," and they were gone. I had never met the man; I had heard horror stories of people who kidnapped babies, but this was a crisis. I managed to get to my room and lay on the bed and rang for a doctor. Soon the Italian doctor arrived. He examined me, then stated.

"You will lose your baby unless you stay in bed. I will give you an enema to help."

I had heard that the Italians' answer for anything was an enema but I knew this was not what I needed.

"No, an enema will not be needed, but I will stay in bed as you prescribed."

I rang the reception and asked them to find a reliable Nanny to look after Fiona; I called Guy Hamilton and Bernard Cribbins and Noel Harrison to tell them the situation, but I did not want them to tell Ronnie yet as he would worry. A capable English agency nanny arrived, even before Fiona was returned to me by my gentleman saviour; Guido had become attached to Fiona and offered to take her out every day whilst I was in bed. I stayed in bed for a week, and was visited by many of the cast and crew and Guy Hamilton was kind and considerate. When the danger of losing the baby was over, he contacted Ronnie to assure him that I was now well again. All expenses for the nanny and the doctor would be paid for by the production company.

We returned to the wonderful cool air and rain in England when the studio work was completed. Ronnie wanted to do some theatre work again. He was offered several television plays: *The Probation Officer*, and *The Invisible Man*. This satisfied him, and kept the money coming in until he was given a challenging role at The Mermaid Theatre. It was a double bill of two Shaw plays, directed by Frank Dunlop. Milton Shuman, the theatre critic for the the *Evening Standard*, was not impressed by *Androcles and the Lion*, nor by *The Shewing-up of Blanco Postnet*.

"*Ronald Fraser blusters his way effectively through the Posnet role...*" he wrote. Davy Kaye had better reviews for his part as Androcles. However, Ronnie was happy to be in a play that demonstrated his versatility: he played two different characters every night.

I was booked into the Charing Cross Hospital for my delivery in October. I woke in the night with pains and knew I had to go to hospital. Fiona was staying with my sister, Jean, so all I had to do was to ring an ambulance. I collected my suitcase, which was packed with the items I needed for the hospital. Ronnie arrived at 1:30, slightly drunk.

"Where are you going?" he slurred.

"On holiday. Where the fuck do you think I'm going?" I gasped between nasty pains, which were becoming more frequent, "I'm going to call the ambulance."

Ronnie grabbed the phone and said, "Oh, no you are not, I will drive you."

He piled me and my suitcase into our tiny Austin Seven and we swerved down the road. I was terrified that I might have my baby before we reached the hospital, also scared of Ronnie's erratic driving. We made it just in time. Alison, our second daughter, was born naturally and quickly. Ronnie tried to compensate for his drunken driving by asking the nurse if he could stay and hold my hand during the birth, but he started to feel sick and had to be ushered out of the delivery ward!

Alison was a replica of her father with a round face and blonde hair. She was a docile and easy-going child, unlike her sister. We had bought Fiona a life-size doll when she returned home, suggested by the experts to avoid jealousy on the arrival of a new sibling; Fiona promptly took the doll and threw it out of the window. She would also undress Alison in her cot and I would wake to find a shivering, screaming child, blue with cold in the winter mornings.

We decided to employ an au pair, not just to help me with the children, but to have a built in baby-sitter so that I could go out at night to join Ronnie and his friends. I found Virpi, a gorgeous Finish girl who adored Alison and did not mind the spartan conditions in our tatty Kilburn flat. Alison was christened in the same church in Hampstead where we had been married. James Villiers was her Godfather and Elfrida Eden and Derina Newell the godmothers. The reception was held in our flat. My parents were there and many actor friends crammed into the tiny living room, raising glasses to Alison's health. It was Virpi who noticed that Alison was hot and had a crop of little spots on her face. She had chicken pox! I did not tell the guests, as I knew it was extremely contagious, but removed the poor darling into another room and left Virpi to care for her, with the excuse to our guests that Alison was tired.

When Ronnie finished in the play at The Mermaid, he had a break, so we decided to visit his mother in Ashton-under-Lyne. She had not seen her second grandchild. Ronnie was now well known in his home town and the locals turned out to greet him as we went into his mother's home. Annie was proud of her famous son and thrilled to see Alison. His mother had the kettle boiling on the fire, everything was spotless in the tiny house, and she wanted to hold the tiny Ronnie look-a-like immediately.

"What a wee beauty," she cooed. "She looks like her father without a doubt."

I refrained from pointing out that Alison did not have a broken nose.

Annie would hold Alison in her good arm and would prod Fiona with the stump of her other arm when Fiona touched her sister too roughly. Fiona was terrified and her grandmother used to say, "Don't you worry. It's only a wee bit shorter than the other arm- but it's every bit as good." There was a constant stream of friends and neighbours who turned up to see Ronnie and the children, all wanting to hear from Ronnie about the film stars he had worked with. Annie revelled in Ronnie's popularity and success and I grew to love this extraordinary woman who had struggled with her infirmity, yet managed to produce a talented, likable son.

Ronnie had been offered parts in two television plays: *The Lonesome Road*, by Giles Cooper and *Sealed with a Loving Kiss*, by Galton and Simpson. In both productions Ronnie played completely different characters and received excellent reviews. In August he appeared in the play, *Purple Dust*, by Sean O'Casey, again at The Mermaid Theatre. The play was panned, but Ronnie received a favourable mention. "… there is always the irreplaceable Ronald Fraser to beguile and amuse us as the most eccentric Englishman you ever (or never) saw."

In every production he worked in, he would make new friends. "I met this fabulous, amazing, interesting actor," he would recount; I believe that actors use the nomenclature "darling" to everyone they meet, because in a play, film or television they work with many different people, but if one works in an office you see the same people every day. I am guilty of gushing, "darling" when I can't remember a persons' name.

The film of *The Pot Carriers* was finished in 1962 and was to have the premiere at the London Pavilion Cinema. Ronnie had his name above the title, proof of his talent and popularity. I wore my little black dress again; it was quite low cut in the front so I stuffed a pair of tights into my bra to get some uplift. Ronnie had on a dinner jacket and, although I would not have called him handsome, I was proud to be with my broken-nosed, beaming husband. A studio car collected us from our flat and we arrived at the cinema where crowds lined the pavement and photographers flashed their cameras at us in the foyer. I smiled and smiled, then looked down and noticed that my tights were hanging out of my décolletage! Mortified, I turned away and pushed them back out of sight.

The celebratory dinner was held at the Cafe de Paris. Champagne flowed and I tasted snails for the first time. Davy Kaye, also in the film, had brought Tommy Cooper with him; they had been a double-act in the Music Halls many years ago. Tommy Cooper had his own TV show and was one of the funniest men I had ever seen. Meeting Tommy was the highlight of that evening, a huge man with a huge personality. We met him many times afterwards, because Davy had a Christmas party every year to which we were invited. Tommy would do a skit with Davy, *The Long and the Short...*, which had us in hysterics. His death on stage was a tragedy, but his comic magician act will last forever. I watch his DVD's now when I want to laugh.

In 1963 Ronnie appeared in several unmemorable films, but he was earning about seven thousand pounds a year – and spending it! Night after night we would dine at expensive restaurants: The Ivy and The White Elephant on the River were the favourite haunts of actors. When we first married I could not cook, so Ronnie gave me a cook book, *The Crosse and Blackwell Cookery Book*, where all the recipes were from tins. I made Corned Beef Hash for us at home and this became Ronnie's favourite. The White Elephant published a book of actors' chosen dishes; Corned Beef Hash was Ronnie's entry.

Liz Taylor and Richard Burton made a film set in London called, *The V.I.Ps*. The film, directed by Anthony Asquith, had an impressive cast: Orson Welles, Rod Taylor, Louis Jourdan, Maggie Smith, Margaret Rutherford and Ronnie. The plot centred on a group of V.I.Ps en route to New York, who were stranded at London Airport because of a fog. It was rumoured that Anthony Asquith chose Sophia Loren for the female lead, but Liz Taylor was scared because of the known appeal Sophia Loren had for Burton. Liz Taylor persuaded Asquith to cast her in the role instead. The film was mediocre, despite the cast, but was helped when released by the publicity about the affair of the two stars in *Cleopatra*.

It also gave me an opportunity to meet Liz Taylor, who had been my idol since, *National Velvet*. We had been invited to a party in Hampstead, and there she was! Dressed simply, but those violet eyes reflected her soul; she had star quality but did not flaunt her status. She joined in with the guests and knocked back many drinks, laughed and joked with all of us. Burton once said, "I love Liz because she is one of the boys; she is also beautiful, from the waist up, unfortunately she has legs like a Welsh pit pony!" Obviously her legs did not matter too much, because they were married and divorced twice. Their love is legendary.

SEPERATION

ACT VI

Ronnie's career was flourishing, but our marriage was floundering. I would be awake every night listening for a taxi to stop outside our flat; Ronnie would stumble up the stairs around 2 am and fall into bed in an alcoholic stupor. Sex was a thing of the past. I knew that actors liked to unwind after a show, either at Gerry's Club in Shaftesbury Avenue or at the Buxton. These were clubs that were open late and catered mostly for people in the theatre, but Ronnie's drinking had reached a worrying level. He had a drink named after him – "the Fraser Special" – which consisted of a double Vodka with a kiss of lime and a dash of soda; he could not go through a day without a drink.

My intuition told me that he was having affairs; he had an address book that was full of girls' telephone numbers. The stubs of his chequebooks were crammed with names of expensive restaurants and nightclubs and he would try and hide these from me. I was getting very little money for housekeeping and clothes for the children, yet Ronnie was spending like Onassis.

I did not want to go out drinking and to check his night time activities, because I was looking after two demanding children and woke early to attend to them. They hardly ever saw their father; he would be in the pub when it opened and back home when they were in bed. I took Fiona and Alison and the new mother's help, Mary, to Bournemouth, where my parents then lived, for holidays. We would dig a hole in the sand and put Alison in it, Fiona delighted in filling the hole up so Alison would be covered! It was a relief to be away from Kilburn.

Ronnie's drinking became worse. He became violent and once he dragged me out of bed to clean the flat. I tried to leave him. I answered an advertisement in *The Lady* magazine for a live-in help for an old lady who lived in the country, but she did not want my two children as well. My loving, amusing husband had turned into a selfish, incoherent wreck.

Mary, our mother's help, left; she was fed up with the constant rows and also the damp in her tiny bedroom. I managed to talk Ronnie into finding a house. The children were three and a half and one and a half and needed more space. We found an old dilapidated Vicarage in South Wimbledon. It was vast: six bedrooms, three living rooms and a garden. Ronnie took out a mortgage and we packed up our few items of furniture and left for leafy Surrey.

It was bliss! The children had fun running in and out of the bare rooms and playing in the overgrown garden; I bought some more second-hand furniture and tried to make the mansion a little more homely. I hoped that this change would bring about a better life and improve my relationship with Ronnie. He had three more films to complete and they were all to be shot in England, he did not need to go away from his family.

We had been living in Wimbledon for three weeks, but Ronnie was out every night and when he came back I could smell a strong scent on his clothes. I asked him if he was having an affair; he denied that he was or that he ever had. I just wanted him to tell me the truth. I did not intend making a fuss, but to know that my intuition was correct and then I could deal with the situation. To encourage him to be honest, I foolishly told him about a one-night stand I had had with an actor when I was feeling miserable and things were bad between us. Ronnie got into his car and drove away into the night.

Next day in the afternoon the bell rang, I opened the door to find James Villiers standing there.

"Come in, darling,"

"I'm afraid I have bad news, Lizzie; Ronnie wants his clothes, will you pack them up, and I will take them to him."

"What? What are you talking about?"

"He has left you." James sheepishly said.

I laughed at first, then, looked at James' long face and realised it was true. In a daze, I went to pack Ronnie's clothes and carried them downstairs to give to James, who took the suitcase, gave me a peck on my cheek and left. In retrospect, I wish I had thrown all Ronnie's clothes out of the window and told James, "to go to hell"! I was in shock. I cried and screamed and tried to accept the reality, asking myself, "Why? Was it because Ronnie could not accept my truthfulness last night? Did he not love me anymore? What about the children? Could he not cope with family life and needed freedom to pursue his career?" I realise now that most men cannot accept unfaithfulness in a partner, no matter how many times they have been unfaithful – I was so naive.

I lost two stone and developed a revolting rash all over my body. My friends came to see me and give advice, "You're better off without him. He's an alcoholic; find someone else." But, I could not, I was in love with Ronnie and yet, he had ruined my dreams of a perfect marriage and family.

I let out the top floor of the house to a German woman who had a small baby of mixed race. Gunda would baby sit for me in return for the use of the flat. One day a friend of mine from Australia came to visit me. When he came to the house, there was a large pram outside the front door with a chubby dark skinned baby inside. John had heard about our separation had assumed it was because I had produced another child of different parentage!

I got a job at an escort agency in Piccadilly. These agencies were different to the ones that operate now. You were not expected to go to bed with a man: you accompanied him to the theatre and for dinner and made polite conversation. If he propositioned you, and you needed money, you could go to bed with him, but I found the men boring and unattractive; most were married and it reminded me of how fickle men could be.

Sometimes Ronnie would send a studio car for the children to go to Elstree where he was filming. I waved them off, crying inside, and they would return full of chatter about their day and about their father. I was their stability; he was a glamorous interlude. I felt inferior and useless and Ronnie never spoke about returning, so I decided to divorce him.

I contacted a London lawyer to discuss a divorce; he told me I had to prove Ronnie's adultery and suggested I hire a detective. I did not know exactly where Ronnie lived, only the area. The detective followed a man of Ronnie's description, from South London to Greenwich, only to discover that he had followed the wrong man! It was costing me a fortune to employ the detective so I decided to do some personal investigation about Ronnie's whereabouts.

I met a new friend in Wimbledon who lived up the road. Gerry had two boys about the same age as Fiona and Alison and they played together most days. Gerry was a gutsy lady with her own big problems: her husband was a schizophrenic. She sympathised with me and with my situation. James Villiers, who often came to see me, let slip that Ronnie was living in a certain area nearby. Gerry and I put on wigs – mine was blonde, hers dark – and we drove to the nearest pub in the area James had mentioned. The publican told us that Ronnie lived up the road, giving us his exact address.

We parked the small car in a side road beside the named house, climbed over the fence and forced the back door open. I searched through all the drawers and found proof in writing of Ronnie's relationship with a new girlfriend; I also found bank statements confirming his latest salary. We went downstairs to the kitchen and I saw a large array of booze. "Let's take the bottles; he's got more money than us." We stashed the bottles into bags and left over the fence, our wigs slightly askew. Later I discovered that Ronnie was away and had let his house to John Hurt.

The date for the divorce hearing was set. I knew Ronnie was in America filming *The Flight of the Phoenix*, and I found his hotel telephone number; I thought maybe I could call off the divorce and we could get together again. I rang the transatlantic number and asked for Ronald Fraser's room.

A woman picked up the phone. "Mrs Fraser speaking," she said. "Not bloody yet you're not!" I screamed and banged the receiver down. Next day I swallowed several diazepam pills and, accompanied by two girlfriends, arrived at the law courts. It was final; we were divorced. I was given custody of the children and Ronnie was allowed reasonable access. I was devastated and lonely. Mutual friends had taken sides; most of them chose to continue to see Ronnie, but a few loyal friends tried to cheer me. Sean Connery was one of them. He would take me out to the Buxton Club to show that he cared about my sadness.

I was introduced to a handsome cockney man by an actress friend who lived in East Ham. He was a tally man; driving around in a van selling clothes from door to door. His cockney accent was so strong I couldn't understand anything he said at first, but he had many other attributes. Dougie adored my children, he played with them and took them out for treats; he became a replacement father and we started an affair, so naturally he would spend the night.

Ronnie had returned from America and wanted to see the children. His agent would ring me to arrange a meeting. The studio car would arrive and Fiona and Alison, dressed in their best clothes, clambered in. I felt sure that Ronnie quizzed them about what I was up to and although they were still young, they probably talked about Dougie, their "new Daddy". One night, the vicarage bell clanged at midnight. Dougie and I were in bed together.

"It's Ronnie," I whispered. "Go into the au pair's room – quick."

He scuttled into her bedroom and into her bed to hide. I am not sure how necessary that was? There were other hiding places in the room!

My ex-husband pushed into the house with no apology for the late hour.

"I need to talk to you, Lizzie."

I replied, "Ronnie you are allowed reasonable access, but this is unreasonable access!"

"OK," he said, "but I have been thinking. I cannot go on paying the mortgage on this house; I think you should move to somewhere smaller."

Actually, he was right. I couldn't maintain the house on the pittance he was giving me and I had to think about schools for the children in the future.

"Can we talk about this another time?" I wanted him to leave and was terrified he would go upstairs and find Dougie.

"Right, I hope we can agree." Then at the door he turned and said, "I still love you, Lizzie."

We moved to a smaller town house in Barnes. It was wonderful for the children because it was opposite the common and they could ride there safely on their bikes; schools in the area were good and I had less housework to do! Dougie and I were still together. He would keep a packed suitcase under the stairs in case Ronnie arrived at night. Dougie would exit the back door when Ronnie came to the front door. There was a side gate in the garden.

In 1969 Ronnie was offered a part in *Sinful Davy*, a film to be directed by the infamous John Houston in Ireland. Ronnie asked if I would come over to Ireland with the children and spend some time with him on location. I went. Why? I was still in love with Ronnie and wanted to be with him and hoped we could reconcile our problems.

Another year later, Ronnie had a month free from work and we all flew to Malta. He wore his kilt on arrival, but left it in the villa for more suitable attire when the temperatures rose to forty degrees. We would spend most days at a club with a swimming pool where Ronnie taught the girls to dive.

One day a voice shouted, "Ronnie, my old mate, how are you? It's me, Hancock."

Indeed it was, but a very different man from the comic genius we had all loved from his *Hancock's Half Hour*, show. He was accompanied by a female nurse and a bodyguard. He came to join us beside the pool and waved his hand at a waiter,

"Drinks here, please."

The nurse came up and took his arm, "No, Tony, not allowed," she whispered.

"Mind your own fucking business; if I want a drink with my old mate Ron, I'll have one."

The bodyguard moved in trying to propel Hancock out of the club. The majority of the members who were rather proper expats were horrified at Tony's language. He was virtually dragged off the premises still shouting and swearing. Tony died in Australia some time after this episode. Alcohol had claimed yet another genius.

Our attempts at reconciliation did not work. My deepest wish was to be reunited, not just for myself, but for my children who loved their irresponsible, mercurial father. Then he lied to me. He had found a new girlfriend, but denied he was seeing anyone else. A friend rang me one day to tell me Ronnie was with his new girlfriend and was outside his house. I jumped in my car, drove to the place and tried to run him over! He avoided injury and possible death by jumping over the wall behind him.

I received a letter from Ronnie begging to be forgiven and saying he wanted to come back to me. For the first time in my life I allowed my practical side to overcome my emotions; I said, "No." I did not want more lies or a life where his moods would be dictated by alcohol.

I had separated from Dougie, who now had a new career as a male model; he had removed his suitcase from my house. I met my husband to be at a marriage bureau where I was working. He was an academic and a complete contrast to Ronnie: tall, handsome, intelligent and free. He would come to my house and stay the night. One night Ronnie arrived at his usual late hour and Eric was there, he did not rush out of the back door. Ronnie was taken aback by this resolute man who was not threatened by his arrival.

However, Ronnie wrote to me saying that I should ask, "my new man to pay the mortgage, if he was living in my house".

I married Eric and had a beautiful son, Simon. He was ten years younger than Fiona and Alison. They adored him and would take him out for walks and amuse him. We moved to a large house in East Molesey. Eric was an ideal father to Simon, but he was extremely jealous about my past relationship with Ronnie. He tried to insist that Fiona and Alison changed their name to his own; they knew their real father and refused. Then Eric developed bladder cancer. He went on a punishing diet, "The Gerson Therapy". All food had to be ground in a manual grinder and he had to have coffee enemas every day. I prepared the vegetables and did not go out, apart for shopping, for six months. Then, after discussion with Eric, I decided to go away for a week to Corfu with a friend. Fiona said she would come down from Manchester where she was working to look after Simon. Oh, the relief to be away from my severe daily routine!

I returned after a week to be met by Eric at the airport. He had a black eye and bruises on his face.

"What ever happened," I cried.

"Your husband," he said. "He had me beaten up."

I later discovered from Fiona the true story. She was due to go to a party at Ray Galton's house and Eric had punched her in the face, leaving her with bruises. Ronnie was at the party and noticed her battered face. When she broke down and told him what had happened, he decided on revenge.

Ronnie contacted one of his friends to appear at our house and to threaten Eric, saying if this ever happened again, he would be in trouble. Apparently, Eric hit the man and so he retaliated. Ronnie was hiding in a garden down the road, ever the coward, and they drove off. Eric told me that he would never allow Fiona in the house again. I was not allowed to see her again. I imagined my life without Fiona; it was impossible. I could not accept such a dictate so I said I was leaving and taking Simon with me. Alison was in Canada at the time.

Eric said if I left him he would take Simon to South America where I would never see him again. I knew he would carry out his threat... I spent an agonising year trying to sort out our problem, but I ended up by getting a divorce and moving to a house in South Wimbledon where Fiona got a mortgage and Alison moved in with us. I had never been forced into committing such a terrible act in my life, leaving a beloved child at the age of only seven, but there was no alternative. Simon came to stay nearly every weekend. He was at a good school in Wimbledon and living nearby. I had a feeling that it would not be long before I had him back.

Eric died of cancer when Simon was nine years old. I have written about this in my other book, *Lizzie's Paradise*. I do not feel remorse about leaving him when I did, just an infinite sadness that it had to end the way it did. Eric left all his considerable estate to Simon. The trustees ensured that I was given adequate money to bring him up and he became an attractive, sociable, fun loving, intelligent man and pursued a career in chemistry, like his father.

FAREWELL

ACT VII

I saw Ronnie rarely after Eric died, and Fiona, Alison and I went to live in South Park Road in Wimbledon. I was doing a part-time course in Social Work at London University. Alison was at Art College and Fiona working in the City. Simon went to Kings College School, which was nearby and I had an excellent help who would be at home to let him in after school.

In 1970, Ronnie became a national figure after the television series of *The Misfit*. He played Basil Allenby-Johnson, nicknamed, "Badger," an upright colonial rubber planter, cast adrift in a Britain he no longer understands. The series ran for only thirteen episodes but, "Badger", with his tropical suit and toupee, became a popular character. Hats became Ronnie's trademark, he wore them indoors and out; he was going slightly bald so they were a good disguise.

There were some memorable and unmemorable plays, films and television productions that Ronnie appeared in during the seventies. The biggest mistake was, *Rentadick* – you can imagine why from the title. A TV series, *Spooner's Patch*, was a huge success with Ronnie playing the lead role.

There were other cameo parts including the TV series of *Swallows and Amazons,* which attracted publicity because the boat on which they were filming was declared "a hazard to shipping", in the Bristol Channel.

In 1978 Ronnie flew to Africa to film, *The Wild Geese*, the story of a group of mercenaries who attempted to rescue an African president. The cast starred some of the "Hellraisers" – Richard Burton, Michael Caine and Roger Moore – and they drank heavily, although Burton at that stage refrained as he had been warned off by his doctor. The jungle location was hazardous and humid, increasing their need for liquids. The film turned out to be a huge success and is shown on television every Christmas!

Shortly after Ronnie's return to England, I joined him for dinner with Alison and Fiona. I was shocked at his appearance. His liver was distended, his eyes were yellow, he picked at his food and his hands were trembling when he used his knife and fork. As usual, he amused us with anecdotes and tried to ignore his physical problems. The next day I learnt from Alison that he had been admitted to the Royal Free Hospital for treatment to his liver. After being discharged he continued to drink – only wine, but a lot of it. He was not offered much work, because the word got round that Ronnie was unreliable and could not remember his lines.

In 1981 he went to see the doctor again and was told that he must never have any more alcohol or he would be dead within the year. That was the shock that forced Ronnie to change his way of life completely. What could replace the camaraderie of visits to the pub? How could he lift his depression and anxiety? How could he survive without his old friend, the "Fraser Special"? He found a way.

Ronnie then lived in a large, elegant, but slightly scruffy flat in Belsize Square. The walls were decorated with paintings he had collected from all over the world and he had his beloved grand piano. He tried to go out to the local pub and to drink soda water or orange juice, but without the numbing effects of alcohol he found his fellow drinkers to be boring, telling the same story over again. He realised he had done the same in the past. Peter O'Toole lived nearby in Kilburn; he had also been advised to stop drinking after a serious operation. They found a source of marijuana, or "comical woodbine" as Ronnie referred to it! They would settle down with smokes and watch videos all day. No need to go to the pub anymore just to relax in a haze of smoke.

Offers were infrequent and not of the standard Ronnie was used to, so he changed his agent. In 1991 he was offered a part in a television play by David Conville on BBC 1. It was a two-hander with Ian Carmichael about a couple of retired men in a home who passed their time writing Obituaries. It was a hilarious comedy with a moving and clever finale entitled, "Obituaries."

I am going to quote an article written at that time by Hugh Montgomery-Massingberd because it sums up where Ronnie was in his acting career and to a degree in his personal life…

"I shall be tuning in eagerly to BBC television tonight... because one of the stars, the great and lately under-used Ronald Fraser, is one of my favourite actors... Gaunt and thin, he looked a shadow of the rambunctious Ronald Fraser of yore, that colourful performer, who gave us a definitive interpretation of the absurd Apthorpe in Evelyn Waugh's Sword of Honour, a memorably hilarious Falstaff and who created the retired rubber planter "Badger", with his battered and indestructible dignity, in... The Misfit... After tonight, I look forward to Ronald Fraser bouncing back to where he belongs – among the most accomplished and sought-after upholders of the great tradition of British character acting. Happily his own obituary is a long way off; the very best of Ronnie may yet be to come."

Unfortunately Hugh's predictions did not materialise. Ronnie gave a good performance as a naughty judge in an adaptation of *Moll Flanders*, then nothing. Apart from staying at home and smoking, he would get some fresh air by playing golf. For years Ronnie had tried to perfect his game, but because of having had his legs in irons as a child, his knees gave him problems, so his swing was painful. One day he was playing with Dinsdale Landen at Richmond Golf Club – he took a swing – missed badly; walked to the pond on the green and threw all his clubs into the water!

I had been living in Greece for seven years, where I had bought a taverna and yacht club. I returned to England in 1997 because I had a hospital appointment. Fiona and Alison met me at the airport and on the car journey back to town Fiona told me the distressing news.

"Daddy is drinking again. He went to see a different doctor, who said he could now drink beer."

"What!" I expostulated, "how is he?"

Fiona replied, "OK, because his friend, Chris Evans, has given him a job on his TFI Friday programme, he is playing the Lord of Love and reads love poems in a ridiculous costume with a silly hat."

I believe in destiny, and it was planned that I would be staying with my old girlfriend, Julie, in Belsize Square opposite Ronnie's flat. If he saw me in the street, he would cross the road to avoid conversation. This was hurtful and uncharacteristic. I received a phone call from Alison one night.

"Mum come quickly to the Royal Free Hospital, Daddy is ill,"

I called a taxi and sped through the night to find a distraught Alison waiting in the reception area.

"Tell me all, darling," I said.

Alison tearfully recounted what had led to this situation.

"Daddy was meant to meet a friend of his, Chris, but he did not keep his appointment. Chris rang me and I had this premonition that something was wrong. I told him to ring the police and they came to break the door down; they found Daddy lying on the floor, he had had a stroke. He is paralysed all the way down his left side and keeps going in and out of consciousness."

"Listen, Ali darling," I said, hugging her tightly. "He is in the best place, The Royal Free Hospital, they know his history" – he had been in before regarding his liver problems. "We should let his friends know, just in case he would like company when he gets better, and we will take it in turns to come and visit him every day."

I had a plane ticket booked to return to Greece in two weeks but kept in touch with Alison and Fiona every day to find out how Ronnie was progressing.

Two days before I was due to leave, I went to see him in the hospital. Peter O'Toole was there, or "POT" as Ronnie called him. He was visibly upset and we went out of Ronnie's private room to chat.

"I knew there was something wrong with the old bugger," he said. "I had seen him one day in the pub and he seemed unwell. I asked him what was the matter. 'Oh, It's my kidneys I think, must go now,' and he wandered off. I think he knew he was very ill, but would not admit it."

Yes, I thought, *that was why he had avoided me in the street*. I saw the consultant that day; he was not encouraging about Ronnie's recovery. He explained that the return to drinking had affected part of Ronnie's brain as well as his liver and internal organs. He must have complete rest, and, if necessary, they might have to operate.

I returned to Ronnie's room to find him sitting up in bed with a pretty nurse hovering over him.

"Would you like a glass of Lucozade, Mr Fraser?"

"Only if you will join me, madam," he replied!

The humour and the charm were still there, so he must be getting better, I thought. I had brought him a bag of oranges, which he had always loved, and I peeled them and popped the segments into his tiny mouth; toothless, he spat the pips out to see how far they would go! I kissed his emaciated face and laughed with him.

"I love you, Ronnie, get better soon." I flew back to Greece the next day.

A week later I was woken by the telephone ringing in the night: it was Fiona.

"Daddy is dead," she sobbed, "Please come back, Mum." I packed a few items and made the long journey to Athens where I caught the first available flight to England.

I had many hours on my flight to think about Ronnie and what I would miss about him most. One of his qualities was his ability to enthral company with anecdotes; I suppose because I was on a plane, I remembered one of his best stories. When he was filming *The Flight of the Phoenix* in the desert, there was little to occupy the cast when not working, so Jimmy Stewart and Dan Duryea started a silly game. Whichever one of them managed to say "Good Morning" first, obliged the other one to buy the first drinks.

It got so mad that Jimmy would ring Dan at four in the morning just to score. Finally, Jimmy decided to hire a spotter plane and planned to holler, "Good Morning Dan!" from on high. But Dan got wind of it and had organised the props men to paint in ten foot letters "Good Morning" on the ground. When Jimmy leaned out of his plane with his megaphone, there it was, and the day's bet lost. Jimmy had the last word though: when Dan got back to his house in Hollywood at the end of the filming, Jimmy had organised flowers in the shape of "Good Morning, Dan" all over his house!

I would also miss his humour and the element of surprise that came with his gifts to me. One Christmas he gave me a wind up gramophone with a vinyl record of Frank Sinatra, my favourite singer. On another birthday, he wrapped this huge parcel in fancy paper and ribbon – inside were twenty rolls of lavatory paper. I always used a lot! Whatever he did, he did with aplomb. He played the piano and sang and taught our children songs from all the musicals that were popular in his era. He appeared in two musicals in London: *The Pirates of Penzance* and *High Society*. His interests were all encompassing.

After two gin and tonics, I became a little maudlin (gin does that to me). I was approaching London, the London where I had met this penniless, ambitious young actor – an actor who strived to surmount his social background by playing other people. I thought how interesting it was that at the start of his career he had played rough, tough earthy characters; however, as the years progressed, he modelled himself, probably unconsciously, on his best friend James Villiers. James was from an aristocratic family and was a witty, stylish actor. Ronnie changed his persona and became labelled "A Typical English Gentleman"; these were the parts he played during the last years of his life. He achieved his goal. Now there would be no further need to act a part, he would be a star, up there, with all the others.

Fiona and Alison were devastated; they had never witnessed death before and this was their father. The hospital had decided to operate because Ronnie's condition was not improving, but it caused internal bleeding and haemorrhaging. They were on either side of his hospital bed; he turned his head to both of them.

"I love you," were his last words.

Peter O'Toole arranged the funeral, my children were too distraught to think about practicalities and I was out of touch and upset. The service was held at Christ Church, Hampstead, on the 20th March 1997, a week after Ronnie's death. The church was filled with actors and friends. Sean Connery, James Villiers, Simon Ward, Peter O'Toole and Chris Evans were the pallbearers. They laid the coffin at the chancel and Peter spoke to the congregation in his beautiful, mellifluous voice,

" I have come to pay tribute to my friend – an incorrigible, naughty, noble old son, Ron." Peter continued, "Ron said to me, 'When I pop off, old boy, I want you to recite Grantchester over my coffin, *all of it*. Why Grantchester? Because it's the longest poem in the English Language'.

"… Stands the Church Clock at ten to three?…

…And is there honey still for tea?"

Peter completed his promise and bowed over the coffin. The sound of sobbing filled the church and I wept too, remembering Ronnie's love of words; words that transformed that ugly man into a thing of beauty.

We followed the hearse to Hampstead Cemetery where the newly dug grave was waiting for the coffin to be lowered. The Master Piper of the Seaforth Highlanders was at the graveside and gave a moving rendition of 'Over the Seas To Skye'. Sean came up and gave me a big hug.

"I can't believe it, Liz, It seems like only yesterday that I was at Ronnie's stag do with the boys and we were blacking his balls in the bath! I'll miss the old bastard,"

"Thanks for coming, Sean," I mumbled.

"How could I not…?" he growled, "Now I must go, I have to play in a golf tournament in Spain. Take care of your wee self."

The final moment came when Fiona, Alison, Peter, Chris and I scattered soil over the coffin and we turned away. Chris Evans, in tears, tried to support Alison, but he was visibly distraught and could do little to help her. Emotionally drained, we climbed into the waiting cars to receive our guests at the party in his memory.

The wake was held in Ronnie's flat in Belsize square. I have never seen so many famous actors crammed into such a small space. Chris Evans had put together a video of sequences from all of Ronnie's best films. There was applause and laughter as we said goodbye, He would have appreciated his farewell.

When everyone had left, Alison and I sat on the sofa in a melancholy mood.

'Mum, I am afraid of dying,' Alison cried.

"Darling, you are still young; your Father was sixty-six years old when he died. You have many more years to enjoy life; I'll be the next one to kick the bucket, believe me." And she did.

ALISON – OUR DAUGHTER

ACT VIII

I called her Ali or Ali Boo, except when I was angry with her and then I reverted to her full name. The plump, fat-faced child grew to be beautiful, with long blonde curly hair, green eyes and a slender figure; she had my shapely legs but without my bumpy knees! When she moved, it was like watching a gazelle; as a teenager she became a perfect physical specimen, but emotionally she was insecure, shy and vulnerable.

Ali was only one and a half when Ronnie (her father) left, so she saw him rarely, although she had a loving replacement father in Dougie, my boyfriend. She must have been confused about our separation. I know now that children often blame themselves when a parent leaves, so as she grew older, I explained that her Daddy left because he had to work abroad, but he still loved her. I hoped this would give her more confidence.

Then Ali developed asthma; there were many times when I thought I would lose her as her tiny chest tried to inhale a breath. After my near miscarriage in Rome, I was terrified she might slip away again. The asthma was contained with medication: a puffer, which was always in her pocket. Fiona had eczema when younger and I wondered if these illnesses were a genetic inheritance or were a symptom of their unstable upbringing.

Simon, Ali's half brother, was born when she was ten and she adored him. She would take him out in his pram if he was crying and rock his chair until he slept. She baby-sat for my friends and took in ironing to earn pocket money. Ali developed a self-deprecating humour, similar to mine, and we laughed together – except when she broke her little finger riding her bike too close to a lamppost!

Ronnie was extremely proud of his teenage daughters: Fiona – small, curvaceous, bubbly and pretty – and Ali – tall, sylph like and stunning. He was upset that neither of them had chosen to pursue a career in the theatre, but Ali excelled at art and chose to follow a career in graphics. She did a foundation course at Wimbledon School of Art, and then went on to complete her studies at Esher College. Ronnie by then had a new, much younger girlfriend and they would take the girls on holiday. Fiona told me they fought most of the time and I was delighted.

Fiona, my reliable, hard-working daughter, was paying the mortgage on a Victorian semi-detached house in South Wimbledon so that we could live together. Simon was at school and the trustees were paying his fees and living expenses; I was on a social services pittance whilst studying part-time at London University. I hoped to be able to earn a decent salary as a trained social worker. Life was hard, but fulfilling.

In order to eke out her grant, Ali worked at a Greek taverna in the evenings. She loved the ambiance, the food and the owner who regaled her with stories of life in Greece. Also, working as a waiter was an intelligent, good-looking young man – Daniel. He and Ali developed a close and loving friendship that was to last throughout their lives. Daniel was gay, but had not yet "come out" and was scared of telling his parents in South Africa. Ali supported him through his dilemma; also, because of Daniel's homosexuality, she could allow herself to love him without the complications of a sexual relationship.

The end of term exhibition proved that Ali was competent at graphics; she was determined to go to Greece and packed her ruck-sac, mostly with paints and drawing materials, then set off on the Magic Bus for the Land of the Gods. Her aim was to visit the Aegean Islands because she had learnt about their incomparable beauty, the blue sea and the infinite light that made the Archipelago ideal for painting. Ali met Bambos, a young Greek-Cypriot man, who was also travelling to Paros. He spoke Greek and helped her to discover different aspects of the island and the people. Ali realised she had found, or been directed, to this tiny place: an island where her soul belonged and where her free-spirited personality could exist and flourish in the sun. However her money was running out, so with Bambos in tow, she returned to England.

It was Christmas time and we adorned the house until it looked like Santa's grotto. I had bought a long, second-hand table and eight gilded chairs from an Indian restaurant. We prepared the feast for days, including a nut roast for the vegetarians amongst us. I asked friends to our house who did not have a family. One friend was Gavinda, who was a Sannayasin; he dressed totally in orange. His gifts from us were many packets of orange dye and t-shirts! Bambos upset Simon by suggesting we make a stew of his pet hamster. I had to console Simon and explain it was just a joke – it wasn't. The Greeks will eat birds, hedgehogs and any animal they can catch. We played charades, drank, laughed and collapsed, contented, late into the evening.

Our house was crowded and chaotic. I was attempting to write difficult essays for my social work course – my final assessment included written work as well as placements in the field – and Simon was studying for school exams. Ali and Bambos were working at the Greek taverna and came home very late, usually drunk and noisy. I could not sleep, so I told Ali she must leave the house or change her lifestyle; she chose to leave and move into a flat above the taverna where she could be independent and go to bed late. I could see a pattern developing in Ali, which was similar to her father's, one of constant drinking and insomnia. I did not know what to do.

Spring arrived and Ali and Bambos decided to return to Paros for another season. Ali had forgiven me for telling her to leave the house. We are both Librans, so we need harmony and do not bear grudges for long. Kissing her goodbye, I promised I would come out to see her when I had a holiday. In her letters from Paros, Ali wrote that she had found work doing sign painting and serving in a taverna, in the town of Parikia. More interestingly, to me, she had a new boyfriend, Demitri, who she said was very handsome. They were living together and she wanted me to come out to Greece to meet the new love in her life.

I did not need persuading because I too was fascinated by Greece. Every holiday I would travel there, usually to the Peloponnese on the mainland. I felt a strong connection to the land, as though I had lived there in another life. I vowed I would live in Greece when I retired. My new friend, Joyce, a social worker I had met on my course, came with me. We struggled to find the ferry to Paros leaving from the port of Piraeus. It was chaotic with people pushing and shouting, but we found two seats on the open deck and settled down for the seven-hour sea crossing. The sun was hot, the sea calm and I was thrilled to be visiting the Cyclades for the first time and to be seeing my errant daughter again.

Disembarking at the quay in Paros were hundreds of Greek people holding signs-

"*We have FREE rooms*" and "*Enjoy our family in bed!*" and other such solecisms. A brown and even blonder Ali came running to greet us.

"Mum, Joyce, how wonderful to see you both. Ignore the hustlers – you are staying with us. I want you to meet Demitri."

She was holding the hand of the most attractive man I had ever seen: dark, and handsome with classic Greek features. I had to support Joyce, who was about to swoon!

"*Yeia sou Demitri, ti kaneis?*" I wasn't sure how good his English was.

"Fine, Mrs Lizzie. Welcome," in nearly perfect English as well.

Their apartment was basic. Joyce and I had to share a bed that had a huge dip in the middle, resulting in our becoming entwined and uncomfortable.

After the second night Joyce said, "I'm going to find a hotel. I hope Ali won't mind."

She gathered her clothes together, avoiding a cockroach that was scuttling along the floor.

"No, go for it, darling" I replied, very relieved to have the bed to myself.

We explored the island, hiring a jeep which broke down on the first day, walked amongst the Byzantine churches, climbed the cobbled narrow streets, swam in the crystal clear sea, gazed at glorious sunsets, ate scrumptious Greek dishes with unpronounceable names, such as *kolokithakeftedes*, drank Orgasm Cocktails at a friend's bar and I delighted in my happy daughter's company. Ali cycled everywhere on a bright pink bike advertising her sign painting. In the flat she would lean over her drawing board with the radio playing, thus improving her knowledge of Greek.

Demitri opened a small bar where, at Ali's suggestion, he served baked potatoes with various fillings. The English tourists flocked to the bar and it produced a dependable income for the whole season. I found Demitri to be mostly charming and polite, but he would have the blackest of mood swings, and he was even jealous of the attention Ali gave me (I was only there for a week). I questioned Ali about this aspect of his personality.

"Oh, he's just typically Greek," she replied.

Demitri's father had recently died and his mother, Artemis, was living alone in Athens, so I proffered an invitation for them all to come and stay with me in England when the season finished. Demitri accepted and Ali was thrilled to know of my generous offer.

"I promise I will help you and I won't drink too much," she whispered as we kissed goodbye at the ferry port.

Snow was lying on the ground when Ali, Demitri and his mother, Artemis arrived at Heathrow. Demitri was not in a good mood because at the customs he had been asked to open his suitcase and discovered that he had 500 cigarettes inside. Artemis had slipped them in without his knowledge to give to her other son who lived in London. Demitri had to pay the excess. Artemis had never left Greece before, and she was ignorant of international laws and spoke no English. Ali and Demitri translated for her during her short stay, but she returned to Athens alone. We had informed Olympic Airways that she would need special attention, but they forgot. Artemis did not understand the announcements (all in English), nor the departure board, so she just sat in the lounge waiting for hours. Eventually an official noticed the waif-like lady asleep on a bench, looked at her ticket and phoned us. We raced to the airport and stayed with her until she was through the departures and safely on the last plane to Athens.

We held a fancy dress party to welcome in the 1987 New Year; the theme was film stars. Fiona was a seductive Liza Minelli, Ali a glamorous Marilyn Monroe, Demitri a scowling Marlon Brando, Simon a reluctant Groucho Marx and I dressed as Judy Garland in *Over the Rainbow*. Everyone made an effort to come in costume with some hilarious results. I believe if you look ridiculous at a party you can relax and the mood is enlivened. Midnight chimed and 'Auld Lang Syne' rang out. I embraced my friends and children, happy in the knowledge that they were all settled. Fiona was in a long-term relationship, Ali had her adoring Demitri and Simon was preparing for his university entrance exams and had many close friends. I prayed that nothing would change and that the coming year would bring joy, serenity and health.

ABOVE: My Parents'
wedding in India.

RIGHT: Me aged 4 at
Boarding School.

Above: Julie and me.

Left: In repertory with David Cunliffe.

My Wedding. Ronnie, Sean Connery, & Mother.

LEFT: Ronnie as a baby but with an adult face!
RIGHT: Ronnie doing National Service in the army.

BELOW: Ronnie with drinking friends.

ABOVE: Ronnie in Israel while filming 'Best of Enemies'.

BELOW: Premier of 'The Pot Carriers'. Ronnie & Liz.

LEFT: Filming 'Sinful Davy' in Ireland. Ronnie, Fiona, Alison & Liz.

BELOW: Fiona and Alison, Ronnie's teenage daughters.

LEFT: Fiona Alison and brother Simon.
RIGHT: Alison aged 1 ½ at the studios.

BELOW: Trizonia, Greece, view from balcony.

ABOVE: Alison and her Mum.

LEFT: Alison happy in Greece.

BELOW: Alison's 40th, with Fiona and Simon & me.

SURVIVAL

ACT IX

I was thirty-five when I married for the second time, and Eric was desperate to have a child. I went to my local hospital, the Roehampton, which was part of the Westminster Group, to have a check up. The consultant, Mr Reynolds, called me for an appointment afterwards. He explained that I had a problem with my cervix and needed a small operation.

"We need to cut a bit away," he said vaguely, "just for safety."

I had the operation, which was nothing painful, and continued back to work. I became pregnant soon afterwards and we were delighted. Then at six months into the pregnancy my waters broke when I was at home, I was rushed to hospital. I did not have any painkillers and went into labour almost immediately. One midwife and a nurse attended me during the agonising labour. The baby was quite large and I obeyed instructions about pushing and panting until I felt it slide from my body.

I heard the Midwife say, "Take that thing away," and then I passed out.

The baby was dead and I developed a serious infection because some of the afterbirth was left inside my womb. I nearly died. I recall praying to God to help me, I was not religious, but someone heard my prayer and very slowly I recovered. When I was stronger, I asked the nurses what was the matter with my baby? What had they done with it? Was it a boy or a girl? They were evasive and never gave me a proper answer. I realise that nowadays a premature baby would be given a burial and the mother would be allowed to hold the child, but not then. I was left imagining the worst scenario and had vivid terrible dreams for years afterwards.

My husband had private medical insurance from his work, so I visited Mr Reynolds in his Harley Street rooms the next time I became pregnant.

"My dear Mrs Parker, we have some important decisions to make. You realise you lost your last baby because we had removed some of your cervix. Tell me, have you had many sexual partners?"

"Yes, I suppose so, I enjoy sex if that's what you mean," I replied.

"Ah! Well it has been proven that the more promiscuous you are the more likely it is that you will have this problem with your cervix."

I was absolutely furious at his inference that all sexually active women would be prone to an infection of the cervix (actually medical science has now proved that a variety of male semen can cause this condition. In those days before AIDS, when we did not use a condom, the possibility was greater).

"So, what can I do now?"

'We will give you a Shirodka stitch. That means sewing up the end of your cervix so you will go full term with this pregnancy. I will do it personally; you will be in hospital for three days and then I will remove the stitch at nine months and the baby will pop out!"

Why is it we are programmed to believe everything doctors tell us? I had my cervix sewn up. I went to the Roehampton hospital to have the stitch removed on the selected date; nothing happened.

Mr Reynolds came to visit me and in his usually tactless manner said, "Mrs Parker, because you are rather old, I think we should do a caesarean delivery."

My husband was there beside me and asked, "Can I come in and watch?"

"No, Mr Parker. That is not allowed."

As I was drifting off, blissfully sedated, I heard Mr Reynolds say, "What does he think this is, – a bloody circus!"

My beautiful, healthy son Simon was born by caesarean section in September. I was thirty-seven at the time and my stitches were very painful. After three days a nurse came into my room and in a brusque manner ordered me out of bed; I could hardly move, let alone get out of the high bed. She came back five minutes later.

"Mrs Parker, why are you still in bed? I want you walking."

I wondered if she had ever had a child, let alone a caesarean. In agony, I slid from my bed, took Simon in his crib and wheeled him into the corridor and made for the exit. Several nurses tried to stop me, but I tottered on—

"What are you doing, Mrs Parker?"

"I'm getting the bus home." I replied, "I will not be treated in this unsympathetic manner." And I meant it.

They convinced me to return to my room for the baby's sake, and helped me back into my bed. I was a private patient and the Matron arrived to listen to my complaints.

"I think you need to tell your nurses that they are dealing with human beings, not just a clinical specimen. Do they realise that having a baby changes one's physical and emotional state. At the moment, I am feeling drained, vulnerable and tearful, and in need of tender loving care! Please tell your nurses, who have not gone through childbirth, that it is one of the most traumatic experiences in any woman's life."

We took him home by car. Oh, the joy of having a new baby, the smell of him, the total trust in his huge eyes, the fat cheeks and the folds of soft skin at the top of his tiny body where I could bury my nose and kiss him endlessly. I breast-fed him at night reading Solzhenitsyns' book *The Gulag Archipelago* to keep myself awake. If the author could survive his atrocious experience in Siberia, and with cancer, my problems were nothing.

I continued to visit Mr Reynolds on a yearly basis at the Westminster Hospital and on the National Health Service because I no longer had private health care after Eric (Simon's father) died. Fourteen years later, after Mr Reynolds had done an internal examination, he motioned me to sit down in his consulting room.

"Mrs Parker, we must now do a hysterectomy, and remove your uterus. The cancer has spread."

Cancer? What was he talking about? He had never mentioned the dreaded word before!

"I don't understand, you have never told me that I had cancer."

"Well, why do you think we had to remove part of your cervix, my dear? I did not want to worry you when we could have cut away the malignant cells, but those cells have spread and there is no alternative but to operate, as soon as possible."

He looked in his diary and said his secretary would ring me at home to let me know when I could be admitted, patted me on the shoulder and ushered me to the door.

I stood out in the street dazed and numb. Cancer! The very word meant death to me. Was I going to die so soon? No, if he removed my womb, then the cancer would go. I focussed on this thought and struggled back home on the tube. I stared at the hundreds of commuters wondering if they had ever had cancer and survived and were still going about their daily routine. I wanted to yell and scream, "Tell me it's not true, tell me it is all a mistake; this cannot be happening to me."

Fiona and Ali shared my concern and helped me by discussing my fears; I did not want to worry Simon too much, he had already lost his father to cancer, but I had to tell him about my forthcoming operation and dwelt on the positive aspects. I had a new partner, Arthur, he was married to a woman who had severe arthritis so she could not participate in his love of sailing We had had many sailing holidays together as he was a joint owner of a beautiful yacht; we always took Simon with us, but unfortunately he was sea sick. At fourteen years old he preferred to be on dry land with his computer. Arthur was caring and reliable and I needed all the support I could get at that traumatic time.

I had my hysterectomy two weeks after my consultation with Mr Reynolds. It was performed at the Westminster Hospital. I was in a great deal of pain afterwards, but I recall the worst thing was not being able to go for a shit. The nurses in the public ward were wonderful; they explained that the operation necessitated my having to be cut further along my caesarean scar. This was causing pain, as well as the internal removal of my uterus. The surgeon had taken a sample of cells, from whatever was left of my vagina, and they were analysed to ensure that there was no more cancer; until the results came through, I was to rest.

Mr Reynolds arrived one day with an entourage of student doctors.

"How are we today?"

Why did he say we, I was the only one in the bed? His minions drew the curtains around my bed and he pulled the sheet down to expose my lower abdomen.

"Oh dear," Mr Reynolds remarked as he peered at my suppurating stitches, "I think I will have to retire soon!" He then went into a monologue about why my stitches were not healing and what should be done now to rectify the problem.

"*Hello*, you are talking about me," I wanted to say, but I was overwhelmed by the sheer number of student doctors (all men).

"I'll be round to see you again when your results come through from the laboratory. Until then, keep smiling."

Mr Reynolds did not come round to see me with my results, his registrar did. I do not know his name, but he had a better bedside manner than my consultant.

"I regret to tell you, Mrs Parker, that the news is not good. The cancer cells have spread and we will have to treat you with radiotherapy to get rid of any remaining cells."

"Please explain what this really means," I said, and so he did. They might have to insert a file of radiation inside my vagina for three days and I would have to be in isolation during this time. Prior to that, there would be tests to see that there was no cancer anywhere else in my body.

The mind is an extraordinary mechanism. If given practical information, it will latch on to it and use it to detract from the emotions. Fear was my overwhelming feeling – fear of death, fear of radiotherapy, a paralysing fear – but I asked the registrar if Mr Reynolds could refer me to the Royal Marsden Hospital in Fulham. I knew this was the best hospital for cancer treatment in London and I wanted the best. The registrar said he would pass on my message and I would hear from my consultant in the future. Now I was to have three months off from work and rest.

The voluntary organisation I was employed by was understanding and found a locum to cover my duties. Ali returned to Greece because she had work commitments, Fiona phoned or visited me every day, Arthur was supportive and Simon stoically continued his studies at school. He did not want to talk about my situation. I tried to reassure him of the future, but with little conviction.

I spent the months reading about diets that could help me, and I went to a hypnotherapist to try and give up smoking, but it didn't work. I tried to stop drinking but alcohol relaxed me and made me forget my fear. Three months went by and I still had not heard from my GP about an appointment at the Marsden. Fiona made me contact Mr Reynolds to find out if he had made the referral. I had slipped through the system, but a week after, I had a letter from the Royal Marsden offering me an appointment.

The extremely young and considerate specialist in the radiotherapy department explained what he would be doing. Firstly, he would perform a small exploratory operation to check if I had cancer anywhere else, then, if the results were negative, I would be asked to come to the radiotherapy department where I would be treated in isolation for twenty four hours. The treatment entailed placing a radioactive isotope inside my vagina.

"If you agree, Mrs Parker, we will start next week."

Was there an alternative? I was in the most advanced cancer hospital in the world and knew that only their expertise could help me now.

"Thank you. Yes, I agree."

The preliminary operations were negative, so the date was set for my entry to hospital. I was taken to a small isolation ward with glass all around and lay on my back on a high bed. My legs were propped up on a solid bridge-like support, and then the isotope was placed in my vagina. The nurses told me I would be alone for twenty-four hours, but there was a bell beside me in case I needed them. I was sedated before everyone left the ward. The door closed and the radiation was turned on.

I slept for most of the time, but when I was awake, I pondered over my life and what had brought me to this moment. Indeed, I had had my legs in the air on many occasions, but those were during enjoyable sexual relationships, now I had a cold radioactive phallus inside me. Was this a penance for enjoying sex so much during my life? Why was it that women who bore the pain of childbirth and the discomfort of the menopause and the possibility of cervical cancer should not be allowed to enjoy sex for its own sake? Men did. If I recovered, I did not believe I would ever feel sexual again.

I tried to be positive and to focus on what I would do when I was better. I had dreamt of living in Greece when I retired. I decided I would pursue this dream and contact estate agents in Greece to find out what was available and the price. That would be my goal.

I was discharged from the Royal Marsden after the consultant said the radiation had been successful, but I was to come for appointments every month for them to check on my progress. I was overwhelmed by the kindness and care I received in every department of the hospital. I bought flowers and wine to say thank you on my departure and later arranged for the bank to pay a direct debit towards cancer research for what remained of my life.

A year went by. I kept my appointments at the Marsden and I returned to social work with single parents, but I no longer had enthusiasm for my job, nor energy. I dreaded visiting the bleak council flats in the most deprived areas and checking if the babies were thriving. Instead, I set up a women's centre where my clients could come to see me. I organised self-defence classes, second-hand furniture provision and started a reconciliation centre on the premises. I was fortunate that Welcare (a Church of England voluntary organisation) owned a spacious terraced house with a garage at the back. It was also at the bottom of my road, so Simon could pop in to see me after school.

One morning after a bath, I was looking at myself in the mirror and noticed bruising on the side of my right breast. I called Ali who was back from Greece.

"Can you see anything here?" I pointed at my breast.

"Umm, yes, there is a slight bruise. Mum you must go back to the Marsden!"

I was referred to yet another Oncology Department and was seen by a specialist in breast cancer. Mr Menzies was a small, gentle man who explained that I must have an exploratory operation to discover if there were malignant cells now in my breast. After the operation, he came to see me and I heard the words I had dreaded.

"Yes, I'm afraid the cancer has returned. But try not to worry. I will make a small incision on the right side of your breast and remove any malignant cells; you will hardly notice the scar afterwards. Please make an appointment at reception when you leave."

Fear and anger overwhelmed me again, but the anger was directed at myself. Why was I continuing to have cancer, the *Big C* as it was euphemistically known? Should I change my lifestyle? How could I find a way to combat the cancer in my body? I would wake up every morning and, as I lay in bed, it would hit me – *I've got cancer*. I never wanted to feel that again, I wanted to wake every day with the knowledge that I was free of cancer.

I am not an atheist, I believe that there is some sentient force in the universe, how else does one explain miracles? I attended groups with my friend Gavinda, trying to find the meaning of life and death. These were Buddhist teachings; I know that Buddhism is a philosophy rather than a religion and I accepted the principles of karma leading us to a better after life. *I must have been a very wicked person in a past life*, I surmised, *to have to suffer with cancer in this life*.

I also attended psychodrama training groups, which would enable me to add another qualification in my social work practice. After my latest diagnosis I met a spiritual woman, Sarah, at a session. She was a devotee of Sai Baba, a renowned Guru in India who performed miracles; she knew about my illness and told me this story:

"I met a woman who had breast cancer, who was told she had six weeks to live. She travelled the world to find a cure, and then in England she was told about this man, a Dr Latto, who gave unorthodox treatment to cancer sufferers. The woman went to see him, took his advice and eventually recovered and is alive today!"

I asked Sarah for Dr Latto's telephone number and rang him as soon as I could. I was convinced that this information had been given to me through Sarah from a higher source. God, an angel, call it what you like, but it gave me hope. I knew I had to see this man.

Dr Latto's rooms were in Harley Street. I wasn't sure if I could afford him, but I went for my first meeting in a nervous mood. I had a quick fag in the loo before going into his consulting rooms. Inside it was like a greenhouse, plants and flowers everywhere, mobiles hung by the windows casting shimmering lights around the room. Dr Latto was a tall, grey-haired man with an engaging smile.

He took me to a chair and in a soft Scottish accent said, "Please sit down, Mrs Parker, the smoker! Tell me everything about yourself and why you are here."

My tears flowed along with the words; I told him about my divorce from Ronnie, my struggle in bringing up two young children alone, the loss of my baby at six months, my second marriage and subsequent separation, my guilt at having to leave Simon, Eric's death and the horror of witnessing death for the first time, and now my fear of cancer which kept returning. Dr Latto did not interrupt me once.

"Now I understand why you are ill, Mrs Parker, your life has been full of sadness and stress, but together we will ensure you recover."

He outlined his recovery plan. I was to go on a strict diet: no meat (because of the hormones fed into animals), no fish (they contain mercury), no alcohol and no smoking. He would give me an injection of iscador (a curative product from the Mistletoe plant) every week for at least a year. He gave me a list of the food I should eat and then prepared a syringe containing iscador.

"Roll up your sleeve, we will start straight away."

"How much do I owe you, Dr Latto?"

"Seven Guineas, dear madam. I do not like this new currency!"

I proffered him the correct amount, amazed at the cheapness of his valuable advice.

"Thank you so much, Dr Latto. When can I see you again?"

He consulted a book on his plant-covered desk and wrote my next appointment on a business card, then gently holding my arm ushered me to the door.

"Remember, stick to the diet and learn to let go, and above all, start to love yourself."

I was smiling as I stepped into Harley Street. I glanced at the card Dr Latto had given me, printed at the top was:

Physician, Obstetrician, Consultant Homeopath.

I later learnt that Dr Latto came from a family of renowned doctors and physicians, several of them had treated the Queen and she was looking pretty good on her homeopathic diet! Dr Latto was seventy-five years old, still played squash and frequently beat his sons at the game. What a remarkable example I had found in this perfect gentleman.

I started my diet immediately. It was easy to become a Vegetarian and I am today, but giving up alcohol was difficult. I realised that most of my socialising involved having a drink and my friends were astonished when I refused. I had smoked since I was nineteen, except when I was pregnant, and I thought that it would be a challenge, but when you have a life-threatening disease, you know you must stop.

Three weeks after meeting Dr Latto, I had a biopsy at the Royal Marsden. Although it was a small incision, I was in considerable pain, but when I saw a woman in the next bed to me who had a complete mastectomy and was having prosthesis implanted, I stopped feeling sorry for myself. I stayed on my diet in the hospital and Dr Latto came to see me and gave me my iscador injection. Before I left, Mr Menzies told me he had removed the malignant cells and I was to return in a month for further tests. He would then be able to ascertain if the operation was a success and if I was free from cancer.

I returned to work remembering what Dr Latto had said to me, "No stress, learn to let go." I planned my future. I promised myself that if my forthcoming tests were positive, I would give up my stressful job and move to Greece. I wrote to the only existing house agents asking for a list of available properties at a reasonable price. A letter arrived from the agents with some details about a property, but it was not just a house, it was a business: a yacht club and taverna on an unknown island called Trizonia, in the Gulf of Corinth. The owners were in a hurry to sell, and the asking price was reasonable. I contacted my partner Arthur to discuss the possibility of going to see the property. He was enthusiastic and his yacht was on Charter in Dubrovnik; he could ask his skipper Jim to bring it down to the island. Alison was in Paros and agreed to meet us nearby with Demitri so we could all sail over to Trizonia to view the place. I wrote to the agent saying I was interested and would like to view, as soon as we could find time.

I went to the Marsden for Mr Menzies to perform the tests on me. The tests that would prove I no longer had cancer in my breast, or anywhere else in my body. I had to wait a week for the results. The waiting seemed interminable; I prayed and tried to be positive about the results. Fiona came with me to the hospital and we held hands as Mr Menzies spread his notes on the table.

"Good news, Mrs Parker, you are clear – no more cancerous cells were found."

I hugged Fiona and Mr Menzies and burst into tears. Oh, the relief, the joy of knowing that terrible shadow in my life had gone.

"Thank you, thank you so much."

"Mrs Parker, you will still have to come for checks here every month, but I am sure you will recover."

Fiona and I skipped out of the hospital.

"Shall we have a glass of champagne, Mum, to celebrate?"

"Love to, darling, but I mustn't. You have one and I'll have Perrier water."

I rang Ali in Greece to tell her the wondrous news; she was ecstatic. I phoned all my friends and had a celebratory meal at home with Fiona, Simon and Arthur. The adage "having a heavy heart" is true; mine had been "heavy" for five years and now it flew. I laughed and smiled again. I discussed the future with my family and partner. I proposed handing in my notice and then flying to Greece to join the yacht, so we could view the yacht club in Trizonia. My goal was to buy a house in Greece, but although this was a business, it could be an even more interesting project. I was well again and ready for adventure.

SERENDIPITY

ACT X

We met at Eghion, a port on the north shore of the Peloponnese. Ali, Demitri, Arthur and I climbed aboard *Arion Bleu*, the beautiful Ketch that Jim was skippering, and we set sail for the island of Trizonia. The Gulf of Corinth is narrow at that point with high mountains sloping down to the sea. There are few towns, just small villages scattered along the shoreline. After about an hour, the compass swung to the point on the chart where the island was situated, there was an islet sticking out of the sea between two peninsulas which marked the entrance to Trizonia.

We sailed into a perfect semi-circular bay; to the north there were a few white houses and several caïques moored along the jetty; to the south, a dirt track road wandered between trees, bushes and grape vines, dead ahead of us was a building clinging to the hillside, the only one. I grabbed the binoculars and focused on it.

"That's it, I can see a sign that says 'Yacht Club' can we drop anchor below, Jim?"

The sea was deep and the anchor held as we prepared to launch the dinghy. We piled in and rowed to a small rocky landing mole, tied up and clambered up some wooden steps to the rough track, then turned right until we came to some steep steps.

"This must be it," Ali said. "There is only this entrance. Let's go up."

Our excitement spurred us up the winding steps until we reached the house and the wooden balcony, which overlooked the bay, where we stood and gasped at the beauty of the view.

The blue sea shimmered in the sunlight in front of the house, which had a central position in the bay. To the left on the mainland, was a conical mountain and we could see the stretch of water that divided the island from the mainland. To the left of the house was a dirt track road leading to the village; we later learned that there were only ninety inhabitants. The bay curved round to the right where the track left the shore and meandered up a hill into the distance. Trees and bushes covered the slopes. Nature had created a visual paradise here on this tiny island; just looking at the view soothed my soul.

The owners were in England, but had told us where the keys were hidden. We unlocked the sliding glass door to reveal a long room with a bar at the end and many old converted Singer Sewing Machine tables with wooden rush-seated chairs underneath. At the rear was the kitchen with an old cooker and gas rings and a walk-in cupboard, and then another room with a hatch to the dining room was adjacent to the main taverna room. Through the kitchen was a small living area with a wood-burning stove and a metal pipe, which was meant to heat the room and which hung from the ceiling. A wooden spiral staircase led to the top floor where we discovered two small bedrooms under the eaves and a miniscule bathroom with a hipbath, loo and basin.

Below the balcony, which stretched the length of the frontage, were two storage rooms and another lavatory facing a sheer drop into the garden; the main house was made of brick with a corrugated iron roof; the taverna room and balcony had been added on later. The house and garden were in total disrepair, there were spiders' webs across the windows and I noticed mouse droppings in the kitchen; a hosepipe was curled up in the corner of the balcony and there was no electricity or telephone – but the house spoke to me.

"Come and live here; give me some loving care and you will be happy here."

We sat at the dusty tables to exchange our first impressions. Arthur saw it as a good business proposition and a base for chartering; the bay was ideal for anchorage for passing yachts. Jim felt that there was a lot of work to be done to make it viable; no electricity meant we would have to rely on generators that worked, there were two rusty old ones in the garden. If we were going to live here, we needed to convert the rooms below and spend a lot of money to overhaul the entire building. Ali loved it. She envisaged letting out rooms to supplement the income from the meals. She would be happy to come and live here, but Demitri was not keen. It was miles away from any shops; customers without yachts would have to rely on the ferries from the mainland. How would we manage without a telephone? He would never want to live on such an isolated island!

We walked down the steps to the village to find some food. There were two tavernas and a mini market. A few elderly locals were sitting in the sun sipping coffee and ouzo, they stared at us with undisguised curiosity as we found a table at a taverna by the sea. The inner harbour faced the mainland, a distance of about 600 hundred metres, where the local caïques acted as an infrequent ferry service. Several old whitewashed houses encircled the harbour, a large modern church was prominent on the far peninsular, a donkey was tethered to a stone drinking fountain, large leafed mulberry trees shaded the tiny square and the atmosphere was totally tranquil. This was the Greece of my dreams.

Over a lunch of Greek salad and fresh fish, served by an elderly man in his slippers, we continued our discussion about the possibility of buying the business and making it financially viable. Everyone had ideas. Arthur, the practical one amongst us, was ready to ring the owners and make an offer immediately, but I thought we should sleep on it.

"Look, I believe fate has brought us here, I wanted a house but this place as a business could be the answer. It would give us all work and somewhere to live."

Demitri suggested he stay in the village and talk to the residents, none of them spoke English, he would learn a lot about the island and give us some vital information.

Ali and I walked back to the yacht together as the sun was setting, casting a glorious orange tinge over the mountains opposite.

"I don't think Demitri likes it, darling," I said.

"Mum, I have to tell you, we have not been getting on well for some time. I do not care if he does not want to live here, I love it."

We rowed over to *Arion Bleu* and sat on the deck, gazing at the little house in the dusk until the shadows lengthened and we climbed into our bunks. I was so excited, my head whirled with plans and ideas about the future, but the gentle rocking of the boat lulled me into a dreamless sleep.

A huge bright sun woke us early, so we drank our coffee in the cockpit and discussed our plans for the day. Demitri had discovered there was a water taxi across to the mainland from the village in the morning where we could order a taxi to the nearest town, Nafpaktos. We could visit a public notary, like a lawyer, who would advise us about the authenticity of the owners' rights to the land and the house, then, if we wished to proceed with the purchase, we could phone the owner from the town. There were telephones in Nafpaktos!

"Let's do it," Arthur said. "We can get a mortgage."

"I can sell my house when Simon has gone to university, or let it for a while."

Jim was already being paid by Arthur for his skippering and he could remain on the yacht and do the house up. We would apply for electricity and telephone. I did not include Ali in our plans because I knew she would have to sort out her relationship with Demitri, but I knew she wanted to come and work and help in the yacht club and taverna. Jim rowed us over to the shore and we caught the water taxi to the mainland. The water taxi was an old wooden caïque with a bearded young skipper called Christos, and was the only person on the island who spoke English (he had taught himself from books and watching American films). English was not then taught in schools; he was delighted to know we might be coming to live on Trizonia.

Nafpaktos was about a twenty minutes' drive from the small harbour at Chania where we caught our taxi. The road followed the coast until we reached the town, which was also known as Lepanto. In the olden days, a famous sea battle had been fought in an attempt to defeat the Turkish invaders, unfortunately the Greeks lost. A ruined castle overlooked the harbour, which had historic ramparts and, of course, cafes that circled the small, cobbled streets. We ordered delicious omelettes and talked about our plan for the day. First we decided to find the public notary and Demitri established that the yacht club owned the land, there were no outstanding debts, and therefore it would be safe to make an offer.

We rang Ion, the owner in England. The line was terrible but Arthur managed to convey that we would like the property; he offered less than the asking price, pointing out that it was in very bad condition. After some bargaining he hung up.

"What? What did he say?"

"He agreed to the price (in drachmas then) but he asked for extra for the contents."

"The contents are shit," Ali remarked.

"We haven't checked them all," I said. "We can deal with that later, but it's ours!"

Ali and I hugged each other and Arthur grinned, while Demitri stared gloomily at the sea.

"Come on, Demitri, have an ouzo and cheer up! Today is a momentous occasion in our lives. Two crazy English people have decided they want to come and live in Greece, not just to make money, but because we feel it is our destiny."

In the house we made an inventory, there was very little of worth: no fridge, only a curtain that hung down in the store room, which was dipped in water to cool the area, no beds, and just mattresses on the floor. There were some old saucepans and a few plates, glasses, cutlery, lamps and candles. The trestle tables were the only decent items. Also, most of the chairs needed reseating. We would make a minimal offer for the contents.

We agreed that Jim could make the place habitable and we would send a builder over during the winter to help him; they could live on the yacht and work on the necessary improvements. We needed to apply for electricity and telephone, connect the water to the village supply, buy beds and fix the generators before we could open for business. Of course, all this depended on the sale being successfully completed at the Greek embassy in London.

Ali and I walked up to the top track behind the house to be alone.

"Mum, I definitely want to come and live here and help you, it's a paradise. You know I can cook and I am used to the Greek ways and I can communicate in their language."

"Darling, I know all that, but there will be many problems to solve, like how are we going to live together in such a small space? What will be your responsibilities and mine? I want to come over to Greece, but I cannot do so until Simon has left school and has been accepted into a university, which means you will be on your own for some time. Will you manage?"

"I know I will. You know when I am enthusiastic about something I give my all."

"OK Ali, I have faith in you, but you must sort it out with Demitri, and I hope you are not going to regret ending your relationship."

"I needed to finish it, Mum. I was not happy in Paros and this will give me the opportunity to start afresh."

"New beginnings for us together, Ali. I wonder why we are both so passionate about Greece; do you think we lived here in a past life and have some issues to resolve?"

Ali laughed, "Mum, I am not sure if I believe in past lives but I do not want to live anywhere else – look at this place, it is unsurpassable in its beauty. I am a Libran like you, we need beauty and harmony around us and we have found it."

In England I arranged to meet Ion at the Greek Embassy to sign the contract and pay the agreed price for the house and contents. We went for a coffee after the deal. I asked Ion about building the house on Trizonia and what life was like on such an isolated island? He told me the history of the discovery and development of the piece of land that was now mine.

Ion was Greek, his wife, Smiley, came from South Africa. They lived in England, but, like all Greeks, Ion had a desire to return to his roots. *Romeiosini* is a phenomenon that is particular to the Greek race; a need to go back to their country. They travelled to Greece in a camper van, looking for land to buy and stopped on the mainland opposite Trizonia, where they decided to explore. They walked around the island until they found an overgrown plot with an idyllic view, so they decided to enquire if it was for sale. A Mr Triantafilo ('Rose' in English) willingly sold two strema (2,000 square metres) of his rocky, precipitous land to Ion.

Ion and Smiley lived in their camper van on the mainland in Chania – opposite Trizonia. Every day they rowed across to the island with building materials, there they hired a donkey to carry the bricks and wood up to the land; the donkey eventually collapsed and died. The main house was finished after two years of arduous work. They were content to live in the simple dwelling, working in the garden and enjoying the peace on Trizonia, but sailors who moored below would trudge up the steps to ask questions about the area: where was the next safe anchorage? Where was there a chandlers? where could they get provisions? Ion usually gave the sailors a drink of ouzo and mezze or coffee whilst he answered their questions. One day he realised he was in an ideal spot to open a yacht club and taverna, so he extended the house.

Ion enlarged the house by adding a long room inside and a wooden balcony to the exterior of the frontage where sailors could sit, eat and drink and keep an eye on their yachts below. Good sailors will always carry charts of the areas they are visiting and usually a large book called *The Mediterranean Pilot Guide* (if they were in the Med). This nautical bible includes information about sheltered harbours and helpful hints regarding the land. Ion contacted the publishers asking them to include his yacht club/taverna. A writer from the magazine came to check out the business and agreed to insert the details in the next updated publication. Ion painted a large sign on the roof, so any sailors sailing into the bay would know there was a place to eat and drink. Trizonia became a well-known stop-off point for any yachts or boats sailing through the Gulf of Corinth.

"The only reason we are leaving is because Smiley has to have a serious operation. We loved it there; it was hard work, very hard work, but we were happy and we wish you happiness too."

Ion, the visionary, said goodbye and, as I watched his retreating figure, I hoped that I would have the courage to survive in a tumbledown shack in arcadia.

HALCYON DAYS

ACT XI

I was fifty-seven when I moved to Trizonia. Simon's trustees had bought a small terraced house in Wimbledon for him and he had been accepted at Bristol University to study for an MSc in chemistry. He would come out to Trizonia for holidays and he had Fiona and his uncle in England to contact if he needed advise. I let my house until I could sell it, so I had an income as well as my widows' pension to live on. I sold the furniture Fiona and Simon didn't want, packed a few clothes and a Greek Dictionary (I had been having Greek lessons at night school, but I was certainly not fluent). I said farewell to my friends and family, making them promise to come over to see me for their holidays, and then left for the airport and a new life experience.

I flew to Athens on an Olympic Airways flight. The Greek passengers clapped when the plane landed! Was this a sign that they did not have much faith in the captain? I descended the steps and felt a blast of heat reflecting from the tarmac, smelt the now familiar pungent aroma of pine trees, and knew I was home. It is a journey of at least four hours, if you are lucky, from Athens to Trizonia. I boarded an old bus at Kiffisou Bus Station with a numbered seat ticket, but the passengers sat wherever they wanted. The bus followed the road along the south coast of the Gulf of Corinth then stopped at the port of Rion. We all piled off and boarded a waiting ferry. The bus, cars, lorries and motorbikes drove on backwards with much shouting and gesticulating from the seamen. The actual crossing was narrow, but the sea could be very rough at that point where the currents converged. If there was a strike, the ferries did not sail at all. A beautiful new bridge now spans the sea between Rion and Antirion, which makes travelling quicker and easier.

The bus terminated in Nafpaktos where the local taxi driver, Ileas, was waiting for me.

"*Kalos Irthate.*" ("Welcome").

We drove back along the coast road until we could see Trizonia silhouetted in the sea, distinguished by its three verdant hills; soon we were at Chania where Christos was waiting with his water taxi. I paid a little extra so Christos could take me around the peninsula and past the lighthouse to the rocky landing stage below my house. Jim was waiting with a light motorbike contraption which had a trailer attached. He hauled my suitcase into the Emmett-like vehicle.

"How's it going, Jim?" I enquired as I stumbled up the dry stony track.

"I think you'll be surprised, Lizzie."

"Pleasantly I hope!"

"Yes, indeed" Jim replied.

I clambered up the winding thirty-nine steps (yes, that was the exact number) until I reached the front door where Ali stood, brown and beautiful, her arms outstretched.

"*Kalos Irthate*. Welcome, my darling mother."

She led me to the balcony where I collapsed into a chair, then gasped at the transformation! The wooden floors had been stained, the balcony rail mended and netting placed between the struts so young children could not fall through; the Singer Sewing Machine tables had been varnished and were set outside on the balcony; the windows were clean and there was a sign above the front door reading "*LIZZIE'S YACHT CLUB*". Ali dragged me inside to look at the bar at the end of the dining room where tempting bottles of booze were displayed, the ceiling was bedecked with flags from various sailing clubs, a pair of white lace curtains hung across the hatch into the kitchen and there was a notice board giving information about water taxi times to the mainland and menus printed with an anchor logo, designed by Ali, lay on a small table near the entrance with a large visitor's book nearby.

Inside the living room, newly painted white, were bookshelves, a table and a bed beside the wood burning stove, oil lamps hung from the beams (we still did not have electricity) and rugs were scattered on the stone floor. Upstairs both bedrooms had been painted and the floors covered with cork matting. There were two beds in each room with yellow curtains hung at the windows and basic wardrobes with a hanging rail and some shelves had been fitted into the walls. The tiny bathroom now had shelves around and under the sink and a new shower and protective plastic curtain surrounded the miniscule hipbath.

"Now, the kitchen – my domain. Come and look, Mum, you won't believe the difference."

It wasn't an Ideal Homes showpiece, but it was clean and serviceable. The storeroom had shelving from top to bottom; glasses, plates and cutlery were placed in strategic positions for serving customers; the only fridge (run off of the generators) was near the sinks; the old oven had been cleaned and the gas cylinders sat below the three burners where most of the cooking was done. Ali had order pads hung on hooks above the serving area; she was organised and in her element.

We went down the freshly painted white steps to the lower level below the upper balcony, to find two rooms. One was a living room with a marble surface which had a gas ring and sink, fitted out for guests, next to that was a small bedroom with two beds covered with mosquito nets, a wash basin and wardrobe. Further along the newly built balcony was the loo with a basic shower inside. I sat on the loo seat and marvelled at the view. Talk about a loo with a view! With the door open I could look through the trees to the sun shimmering on the blue sea and watch the boats sailing into the perfect bay. There was no need for a book whilst waiting to do ones daily motion!

Ali, Jim and I sat on the upper balcony with a jug of wine (it was nearly a year since my cancer cure and I was allowing myself a drink again). I praised them for the work they had done on the house and wanted to know what were the priorities, and if there was any business.

"Let's talk tomorrow when you are rested, Mum. You are sleeping upstairs, and I am opposite you. I hope you will be comfortable and sleep well for the very first time in your *spiti* (Greek for "house"). Now I will make you some food."

I watched as the sun set and cast an orange glow on the mountain and the mainland across the straits from the island. I could see this every night of my life from now on, and share it with my beloved daughter.

I did not sleep well. I was awakened in the night by strange scampering noises in my room. What were they? I put on a sarong and went to sit on the balcony where the sun had risen; it was already hot at 8 am. Ali joined me later with a coffee.

"Did you sleep well?"

"No, I didn't. There were some funny noises in my room."

"Yes, I meant to tell you, Mum, we have a lot of mice and rats in the house. We are in the country and I suppose we have to accept them. I don't want to put poison down, so I bought a humane trap. If they go in it, I take them down to the bottom of the garden – but I think they find their way back!"

"We must get a cat." I said.

"We have got one left by Ion, called Kebab, but she is old and lazy and doesn't chase them. You will have to accept them."

I tried, but when one of our friends was staying in the room below and a mouse crept into her long hair one night, we decided to get more cats and to put down poison. Visitors were paying for their rooms and would not return after such an unpleasant experience.

I had applied for electricity when I knew the house was mine and put down the equivalent of £1,000 in drachmas. I was not getting any interest from the bank, so I wrote a letter to the European Union asking them to intervene. They did so, and within two weeks we noticed that a wooden pylon was lying on the mainland opposite. We took the yacht to Chania, tied the pylon to the stern and brought it to the shore below the house. There was a friendly Greek man who operated a digger on Trizonia, we bribed him with the offer of a toy parrot which had a battery up its bottom; when it was switched on it would repeat your spoken word.

Yiorgo coveted the parrot and he agreed to dig a hole on our land ready for when the electricity company arrived to bring us power.

When I lived in England, I took it for granted that if I switched on a light or put in a plug I would have power, when we had that facility in my house it transformed our lives. We could have fridges, lights up the path, in the rooms we could have fans to cool us, ovens, electric kettles and many other necessary items to enable us to run a business, and just for living more comfortably. During the years I lived on Trizonia, I noticed there appeared twinkling lights high on the mountains in villages which previously had been in darkness. I hoped the inhabitants appreciated the miracle as I did.

Ali and I decided on our daily routine. We would not serve breakfast until 11 am. Ali did not like getting up early and we did not get to bed until late if we had customers the previous evening. Lunches would finish at 2 pm, in order that we could go swimming or go to sleep. In the evenings, Ali would be in the kitchen cooking and I was to be the waitress. It should have been the other way round, but Ali was a good cook and she was also shy, so I put on my best servile act (sometimes); although, there were evenings when I could not tolerate the dictatorial attitudes of some customers. I answered back in a jokey way, but made it clear that I would not accept such demands. They were in a tiny island in the Gulf of Corinth, not at the Royal yacht club in England.

In the springtime the flotillas would arrive. We were in touch with their winter base in Lefkada and they would contact us with the time of arrival. This was our big money making period. We would see about twenty yachts sailing into the bay, dropping their anchors and then watch the crew's tenders being launched. We would wait for them to tie up below the house and stand by for the hungry and thirsty sailors.

The majority of the skippers and engineers on the flotillas were Australians. They would come up the steps without any shoes, they were fit and fun and when Ali came out of the kitchen after the meals were over, they were fascinated that such a gorgeous young woman ran the yacht club and would sit and drink and talk with her late into the night. Of course this was good for business, but it meant that every night Ali would be drinking wine until two or three in the morning.

Arthur arrived with a Dell Quay Dory, a Kris Kraf, as it was known in Greece. He brought it from England, towing it behind a second hand Volvo, which we needed for our shopping trips to Nafpaktos. The Kris Kraf changed our lives. It had a forty-five horse power engine and Ali and I learnt how to use it. We would take it over to the mainland rather than use the water taxi, tie it up, go shopping and return laden with essentials. The problem was getting the goods up the steps to the taverna. Arthur and Jim devised a track with a trolley on the top, which could be winched up the steep hill to a place in the garden on the same level as the entrance to the taverna. Our lives became easier: we had electricity, a boat and very soon a telephone line was to be installed, but every day we had the knowledge that we would wake up to the most perfect view in the world.

In our free time Ali and I would go swimming. There were three beaches that we could walk to along footpaths through wild flowers and olive groves. The nearest beach – a walk of about ten minutes away – we called Bottle Beach because there was a lot of flotsam washed up, comprising mostly of bottles. The sea was clean and it was secluded, so we could strip off and swim naked. The other beaches, Dolphin Beach and Red Beach, were a longer walk but they had sand. Dependant on the wind, we would choose where to go. Euripedes said, "The sea washes away all evils of men". I believe him. I felt invigorated and clean after my daily swim and I knew this was part of the therapy I needed to cleanse myself of cancer.

One night we were sitting on the balcony when the house trembled and the bottles fell off the bar. It was my first experience of an earthquake. The lights on the yachts moored in the bay went off and they floundered in the sea. Their anchors no longer held, because the seabed had changed in a fraction of a second. The tremor caused unbelievable damage. Luckily Trizonia is built on rock so there was little damage to our house nor to the village, but on the main land opposite houses collapsed and the road to Galaxidi was blocked with huge boulders, which had tumbled down the mountains. The local radio advised people to get out of their houses and to sit outside. I thought this was ill advised because, if they were outside their houses, they would be a target for the tiles that were sliding off the roofs! The best advice was to run into the sea, as long as there was no Tsunami.

Gradually the inhabitants of Trizonia came to accept us. The owner of the mini market and his family adored Ali. Thanassis, the son, asked her to do a sign for his taverna and when Ali ran out of food (if we had unexpected customers), he would supply us with provisions. Everyone on the island had a boat, just a small caïque with an outboard engine, but they knew the sea and the currents, and the captains of the water taxis would go across to the mainland no matter how bad the conditions were. Some nights Ali and I would go to the village in the Kris Kraf for a drink if we had no customers. It was politic to spend money in another taverna or bar. After several glasses of wine we would get back into the Kris Kraf, accompanied by two captains, Christos and Yiorgo to whizz across the bay to our place. Ali insisted that she was the captain of our boat and pulled the starting cord at the stern, then fell over backwards into the sea. We fished her out and argued who was going to be the captain now. I did not insist on my seniority that night.

Yachts from all over the world would moor below in the bay and come to the taverna for a meal and drinks. Some of the sailors were experienced and had sailed single-handedly around the world; others were novices and only had maps of the coastline and knew little about where there were dangerous rocks or shallow water. They shared their experiences of sailing and joined their tables together to get to know each other better. After a few too many drinks, they did not seem to notice that they had to wait for a long time for their orders to arrive, nor were they phased by the power failures;

sometimes a rat would appear and run along the balcony rail and, as most of the sailors were slightly inebriated, they only saw the rat out of the corner of their eyes. We would say, "That's a lesser-known Trizonia squirrel!" We gave them our Visitors book to sign on their departure. My favourite inscription was from an English man, who wrote- "This place makes 'Fawlty Towers' look like Claridges!"

Ali and I spent a lot of time together in the evenings waiting for customers to arrive. We discussed future plans for the taverna and how to improve the building. Because the floors and ceilings were made of wood we could hear every noise wherever we were. We decided not to have paying guests below, but only let our understanding friends come to stay. There were many of them. Ali was compassionate and a good listener, she remained loyal to all her friends. Although then we did not have the Internet, she would write or ring them frequently. Men were attracted to her, not just because of her looks, but for her ability to understand any problems and to discuss them fairly. She never flirted, which was an admirable quality, and she usually had long-lasting relationships.

Ali's latest boyfriend was an Australian engineer from one of the flotillas called Glen; he returned through the Corinth Canal delivering yachts to the Ionian Islands, and would entertain us with stories of incompetent crew and the hazards of having women with long hair on the yachts who blocked up the drains after shampooing. Glen loved Greece and decided to apply for a job in Skiathos, a small island in the Sporades, where he would have a permanent base. He also hoped that Ali could come and visit him there, if she was not working. I did not know when that might be because I was not prepared to cook in a sweltering hot, basic kitchen on my own!

In the winter we closed. There were no flotillas coming through at the end of the season and it was not practical to be open for a few hardy sailors, also the house was not built for the cold weather. The mountains around the Gulf of Corinth were capped with snow and although we never had snow, there were severe frosts at night; we had one wood burning stove and a few miniscule electric heaters, so we boarded up the doors and windows and left for Australia.

Ali went to Sydney to meet Glen's family and I visited an old friend of mine in Queensland. Jill lived in a tiny house on the edge of a brackish lake with her husband, John. The humidity was intense and I found it the most dangerous place to be. There were revolting spitting toads, spiders that came up the loo to bite you and, worst of all, there were sharks in the sea. There were miles of beautiful beaches, but you were not allowed to swim. I was so used to plunging into the sea wherever I was in Greece that I longed to return to my little paradise.

Ali and I met up in London and then flew back to Athens. We chattered all the way on the bus journey and she told me that she still liked Glen and Australia. Ali had made many girlfriends in Sydney, many of them wanted to come out to Trizonia and some mentioned staying for a while to help her in the taverna. I was pleased to know that I would not have to be the only, rather old, waitress.

The water taxi brought us round to the bay below my house and we were shocked to see the change on the seafront. There were large blocks of cement laid out on the village side, forming a marina! Christos, our skipper, told us of the events we had missed.

The Mayor had received a European Union Grant to build a new marina. The diggers had been working all winter to deepen the seabed. When the divers and engineers had completed it, there was a local ceremony to inaugurate the event. The largest Caïque sailed in to tie up to the new moorings; everyone applauded, but yachts have a much deeper keel than the local fishing boats and it was not deep enough – they had to start all over again!

Trizonia was overwhelmed with strangers (*xenos*) working on the marina. There were Polish, Albanians, French and Greek engineers who would come up to the yacht club occasionally. We should have been pleased with the extra business, but the peace was shattered. A huge dredger and crane were permanently moored opposite on the left of the bay; cement mixers trundled along the quayside all day and a tugboat towed girders into position, creating a big swell in the bay. We realised that, if and when the marina was finished, most of the yachts would moor down in the marina rather than anchor below the yacht club, thus making it less attractive to walk half a mile to dine at my place. For sure the visiting "yachties" would eat in the village tavernas.

Ali decided we needed some changes to make our place more attractive, so we printed flyers to take to the mainland and pinned them on the lampposts on the way to the village. She offered special meals: a Sunday roast, Thai and Indian food (not to be found anywhere else in the vicinity), and happy hour, where cheaper drinks from six to eight were available. Ali had been elected the Commador of the nautical area of the Gulf of Corinth by the Cruising Association in England, so the yachties would come to us for information. We also had a Book Swap service; customers would bring four books and take away three from our packed shelves. This also kept Ali and I supplied with reading material.

The island became more developed during the years we were living there. On the plot of land next to us, two prefabricated houses were built. They were owned by Greek families: two doctors and their children from Athens. They would visit at weekends and borrowed electricity from us until theirs was installed. Behind us on the hill, a French couple who had discovered Trizonia in their yacht years before us, were building a house. On the west side of the island another French family were building a large stone house. A group of French men who specialised in a type of stone wall building were based on the island. In some ways this benefited our business, because they appreciated Ali's cuisine, but we had an ongoing battle with them about who would find and pick the island's natural produce.

The soil was mostly stony, but there were wild mushrooms, asparagus and dandelions pushing up into the sunshine. On the beach we found capers and there were sea urchins, which the French considered a delicacy, but these were very difficult to gather without risking a nasty spike in your skin. Ali and I would take the Kris Kraf over to the small island opposite where we would fish for clams and cook them on a wood fire on the pebbles. We should have been very healthy on this diet, but most of it was undone because of the late nights and our excessive drinking.

It was inevitable when the customers bought Ali a drink, after she had cooked a meal, that she would accept and share some time with them. However, I noticed that she had a glass of wine beside her in the kitchen whilst she was cooking. Her behaviour became very erratic and she would order me out of the kitchen, even though I had a reason to go in to verify an order. I was not a good example, as I was drinking again, but I worried about the genetic influences of alcoholism. I had read that a child was more predisposed to the problem if the disease ran in the family; that half the risk comes from our genes, but also from the environment and availability factor. All these factors were present in our current lifestyle. I watched and waited.

The roof of the room that had been added on to the house had leaked since we moved in. It was made of corrugated iron and there were holes everywhere. Greece is prone to violent rainstorms and at such times we strategically placed buckets underneath to catch the overflow, but we needed to replace the roof. Ali knew of two builders in England, who said they would come over and mend it if we paid their fares. We bought their tickets and expected them in two weeks.

Gary and Fred started off well by stripping the old roof, but they obviously thought that they were going to have a holiday whilst in the sunshine. They finished work at 2 pm and went down to the village tavernas for several beers. Ali prepared them an evening meal, accompanied by more beers, then they crashed out in the rooms below for the night. I had ordered the replacement corrugated roofing from the mainland and it was due to arrive at the jetty opposite on a set day. The builders were supposed to go and pick it up with a water taxi and bring it round to below the house. They were late. There was a very strong wind on that day and half of the roofing blew into the sea, creating holes in the new corrugated iron. I had to order more.

The roof was completed way over the time specified, but it still leaked! Ali and I were so glad to get rid of them, we did not complain. I decided it would be cheaper to use local help in the future and to ensure the employee did not have a drink problem.

I decided to move below to have more peace and privacy. Also, Ali thought it would be better for business if she had a young and pretty waitress to serve the resident lascivious French workers and any other customers (mostly male). I did not object. I was fifty-seven by then and, although very fit, I knew that a young girl was more pleasing to the eye and could encourage customers to spend more in the taverna. There was always a string of Ali's friends from England or Australia who welcomed the chance of a job on a Greek island.

Most evenings I would eat upstairs in the taverna. I only had a two-ringed gas burner and it was very hot below with the low ceiling. One night, after sharing the company of the Polish Marina workers, I said my "goodnight" and went to go down the steps to my rooms, when I noticed a shadow below the fir tree by my door. It was a snake and a huge one, blocking my entrance!

"Oh, God! Help me, I'm not going down there."

Andrea, one of the workers, peered at the reptile and laughed, "No problem, Lizzie, we have them a lot in Poland."

"Get rid of it, please." I was terrified.

Andreas found a thick stick and crept down the steps and with a hefty swipe knocked the snake from the path and lifted it into the garden below. It was at least three feet long!

Snakes were numerous on Trizonia. They would swim over from the mainland and bask on the rocky soil in the springtime. It was the small ones that were deadly. We bought an antidote from a Gypsy in Nafpaktos in case we were bitten. I never walked without a stick and stout shoes after that incident.

My move to the rooms below did not bring me the peace I anticipated. At night I was kept awake by customers who sat at the old Singer tables on the balcony above my head, using the treadles as though they had to finish some work before dawn!

The next catastrophe happened when I was actually asleep. I woke to the sound of rushing water and as I reached for the lamp, my hand dipped into a foot of water. I paddled through the water and climbed upstairs where Ali and two sailors were sitting.

"I need help, or I am going to drown," I cried.

I explained the problem and luckily the men were practical (all sailors need to be able to fix emergencies whilst sailing). The water pipe bringing us our supply from the village had burst. It ran behind the house; they turned off the water at the mains and squeezed behind the house to temporarily repair the pipe. It was three in the morning. I offered free drinks to my saviours and collapsed into a dry bed upstairs.

This episode spurred me into making the decision to sell the yacht club. I was getting older and found the strenuous life difficult to cope with. Arthur could barely get up the steps to the house, our yacht charter was not making money and there was always a huge outlay on *Arion Bleu* just to keep her in the water. Additionally, termites were gnawing away at the timbers that supported the building and wasps had built a huge nest under the foundations.

I discussed my decision with Ali and Arthur. Ali was naturally upset, but she realised why I had to leave. For seven years we had struggled to make the business a success and Lizzie's Yacht Club was known in yachting circles all over the Mediterranean; Ali worked hard and would not be defeated by the numerous problems we encountered, but she was still young and had more energy, also she loved the island.

Arthur agreed to close the charter business and would think about selling *Arion Bleu*; if and when we sold the place, we would split the sale and pay off the mortgage. Jim began working for the Frenchman who was building a house on the other side of Trizonia and had his own small house, therefore Arthur did not need to pay his wages as our skipper.

Ali took my hand as we sat on the balcony looking at the incomparable view. I was close to tears.

"Mum, I know we argue often, but please do not move far away."

"Darling, of course I will be nearby. I might travel a bit, maybe on cargo ships, but I will always come back to Greece."

"I love you more than my life, Mum, never leave me."

REGRESSION

ACT XII

I put an advertisement in the Yachting Monthly magazine:

"FOR SALE – Thriving yacht club/taverna and house in Greece."

I had an email from one prospective purchaser who wrote that he would like to view the property as soon as possible. He was a yachtsman called Bill and had visited Trizonia in the past, so he knew the area and the position of the yacht club. We arranged a date for him to visit; he would come with two friends, one was a Cypriot who spoke Greek and could help with any language problems.

I booked the visitors into the only hotel on the island for their stay. Ali and I rushed around tidying up the house and garden.

"There is no need to tell them about the termites and wasp nest Ali," I said, "Nor the leaking roof."

"Mum, you must be honest with them from the start, they will find out anyway after a survey."

Ali had a really strong moral code – not in the conventional sense of "morals", but she had a strong sense of what was good and bad. She refused to be complicit in anything she thought was bad or morally questionable.

"Well, if it rains they will find out about the roof, but I am not going to mention it."

It did rain on the day the three men came to view the house. They were journalists and had been friends for years. Bill was a tall, attractive and charismatic character, intelligent and with a wonderful sense of humour. I noticed that he was impressed with Ali's looks and forthright personality and I thought, *Hmm, perhaps I can sell my daughter with the business!*

Mike, the Cypriot, was dynamic and shrewd and Tony, the third member, was gentle and kind. We showed them round the house and then took them into the back room, where the roof was not leaking. Ali offered them ouzo and wine and the atmosphere became relaxed as the questioning started. Bill had a yacht in England and had sailed around Greece alone when his marriage had broken down. He had a son who was at boarding school in England. He lived in Nairobi where he ran a Radio station and edited a local newspaper. Previously, he had worked in Fleet Street with a national daily newspaper. We arranged for them to come back the next day, so we could show them the land and answer more questions.

The sun shone on the day after, and Trizonia looked perfect. Ali and Bill decided to walk round the island together; before they left I took her aside and whispered, "Be nice to him, Ali."

"Mum, I know what you are up to. You are hoping if he falls for me he will buy the yacht club. Well, I rather like him anyway!"

I stayed with Mike and Tony and answered more questions and let them wander through the house and garden.

"What are those signs on the steps?" Mike asked.

"That's where customers fell into the cacti after a heavy drinking night," I answered.

Ali cooked a delicious meal on the third evening and luckily some yachts moored below and the owners came up to eat with us. Bill gazed at the tranquil bay and the moon rising behind the mountains, then turned to me, "I love it here, Lizzie, I want to buy it."

"Yes, Bill, I understand; this view feeds your soul. I want someone to live here who appreciates the tranquillity of this remote island. Shall we drink to your happiness? I accept your offer."

"Where is Ali? Come out of the kitchen you gorgeous woman and celebrate with us."

Bill strode into the kitchen and dragged a flustered and dishevelled Ali out to the balcony.

"Raise your glasses, everyone, to a new ownership and a continued successful business."

Bill looked into Ali's eyes as he lifted his glass of wine and I knew that he wanted her, as well as the taverna.

The practicalities of signing the agreement were sorted out by Mike in Nafpaktos with the lawyer, and they transferred the agreed price into my bank. Bill said he would return in two weeks to discuss any other issues. First we had to talk about who was going to run the yacht club. Bill could not live in Trizonia all the time because of his job in Kenya. He was keen for Ali to continue to work in the taverna, if she managed the running of the business, but he would not charge her any rent. Ali was happy with this arrangement and even happier with her new relationship.

What is attraction? Is it chemistry, lust or a more profound meeting of souls destined to live through another reincarnation? I still do not have the answer, but Ali and Bill were besotted with each other. He came back to Trizonia to complete the transaction on the sale of the house. He attempted to help as a waiter during his time in the taverna, but was hopeless in the role. However, he entertained the customers by playing his guitar and charming the clients. Bill and Ali agreed that he would return to Nairobi and she would fly out to Kenya in the winter when the yacht club would be closed.

I was allowed to stay on in the rooms below and then, next year, I would find a flat on the mainland. I knew that it was time for me to leave Ali to run the business. We were so close, both free spirits; yet she was a projection of me, and she desperately wanted to find herself and separate herself. When customers came up to Lizzie's Yacht Club, Ali would greet them at the door, "Hello, are you Lizzie?" they said.

"No, I am Alison, her daughter," she replied.

I had some badges made for her to wear which stated:

"ACTUALLY, I AM ALISON!"

***

We locked up the house in November, letting the snakes, rats and mice have a free run and booked our flights; Ali to Nairobi and I to England.

"Mum, would you, Fiona and Simon come over to Kenya for Christmas? Bill has a big house and said you would all be welcome."

"I will ask the others," I said, "It sounds like a great idea."

As I struggled down the steps with my suitcase to the water taxi, I realised that I was leaving the house which had been my home for seven years. Despite the difficulties and many challenges, I had enjoyed most of my time on this beautiful remote island. I would not move very far away, but it was time to leave.

Fiona, Simon and I arrived in Nairobi on the 20th of December. Ali was waiting for us with a chauffeur driven car.

"This is James," she introduced us to the smiling black driver. "He takes us everywhere."

I detected a note of sarcasm in her voice and waited for the time when we could be alone to discover how she was getting on in Kenya and with Bill.

The house was imposing, but there was a security alarm at the entrance and an iron gate at the bottom of the stairs to the bedrooms where another alarm had to be entered before we could proceed to our rooms.

We sat in the verdant tropical garden beside a large swimming pool and sipped cocktails in the twilight; the warmth of the African sun was a welcome change after the English December climate.

"How lovely this is," I said.

"No, it isn't," Ali replied. Then she told me about her dissatisfaction.

In Nairobi she was not allowed to walk alone in the town, as white people did not go anywhere on foot; James, the driver, took her wherever she needed to go. There was still a big discrimination between black and white people. When she and Bill went out, they only socialised with expatriates and she missed the freedom found in Greece.

"I can't live here, Mum. Bill and I are not getting on well, because I am unhappy with the restricted lifestyle. We have discussed the problem and we have agreed that I must go back to Trizonia alone to run the yacht club. He still has a job here which he enjoys and he is used to the way of life. I think he needs to be the Big White Boss!"

Despite the tension between Ali and Bill, we had a hugely enjoyable Christmas. There were DJs from the radio station and Tony's likable sons joined us for lunch; afterwards, we played a revealing game of "Tell the Truth" during which time I learnt many untold secrets about all my children – and they about me! We drove to Mombasa for New Years Eve and celebrated at Hemingway's, the famous Club where the notorious writer spent his time fishing and drinking. I had a disastrous fall at twelve o'clock when the lights went out, and I missed a step and landed on my knees. I was not pissed, although my children thought I was. Ice packs were called for and I had the worst, agonising three-hour car journey back to Nairobi, and then a flight to England, when the Kenya Aircraft had to return to base because of a shattered windscreen! I was more than happy to be leaving Africa.

I returned to Greece in the spring to find somewhere to live. In a small village of Marathias, only ten minutes along the mainland coast from Trizonia, I found a furnished attic flat to rent with a large roof terrace. It was right on the sea and I could see the island from my windows. Jim came with a tractor and trailer to the yacht club where I had packed my few belongings. We rattled down to the village to get the water taxi. At the bottom of the hill we were accosted by a French couple.

"Is that rubbish in your trailer?" they enquired.

That remark made me realise how cathartic it was to leave my possessions and house. I would rent from now on. I had money from the sale of the yacht club and would no longer have to worry about leaking roofs, termites and snakes.

Ali arrived in Trizonia a few weeks later. I was concerned about her physical appearance when we met: she was thin and pale and her hands shook when she held her glass of wine. I knew she used an atomizer to counteract her asthma, which resulted in shakiness in the limbs, but I suspected that her excessive drinking was now a contributory factor. Ali also had irritable bowel syndrome. She had been hospitalised and checked for this condition when she was younger, but there was little improvement. However, it was her legs that were now causing her pain. She had developed varicose veins, probably as a result of always being on her feet when cooking and waitressing. We had sought advice in England, but an operation was not possible because she had to run the taverna for Bill for the coming season; Ali did not have faith in the success of an operation anyway.

I suggested she employ a stronger person to help in the taverna, particularly with lifting and carrying the heavy beer crates, but she said she could not afford help until the business improved.

"I will come over if you need me, but I am not strong enough now to lift the really heavy stuff, Ali."

"I know, I know, Mum. Thanks, but someone will turn up." And they did, for a while.

There were a succession of sailors who were captivated by Ali's looks and charms. They would rally round and help her with essential tasks, often delaying their planned journeys and mooring their yachts in the bay below, hoping, I presumed, that they would be chosen as her lover rather than a handyman. Ali was still in love with Bill, but their relationship could not sustain the long periods of separation.

"I know he has got another girlfriend, Mum," she confided one evening. "My intuition tells me so, and his voice is different when he phones me. I will run the yacht club for him, as I promised, but we are no longer a couple."

I heard the sadness in her voice and I wanted to hold her and make it better as I had when she had fallen and was bruised as a child, but she was now a grown woman and had to deal with losing her love in her own way, as I had when her father left me. I knew exactly how she felt and would be beside her to give her support.

My daughter was loyal, brave and courageous and despite the problems with her legs and the strain of running the taverna, she was determined to show Bill that she was reliable. He charged her nothing for rent, but she had to pay bills and the costs of everything else towards running the business. I came over if she had a flotilla and needed help with serving, and we would meet in Nafpaktos when she came to do the weekly shopping. We would have lunch together in a fish taverna by the sea, which she loved and where she could relax. Getting the provisions back to the house was a major drama: first, the things had to be unloaded from the car into the water taxi, then loaded into a tractor owned by Nicos, a local man; then they would have to chug up the top road to the back of the house where they had to carry the shopping down many steps to reach the yacht club. It was exhausting and one needed to be fit. The pulley system we had installed had broken.

After the tragic death of her father Ali was financially better off. He had left his large flat and his money to be shared between his daughters. Ali invested in a flat in Surbiton which she rented out and received a steady income and which boosted her living expenses. I hoped this would make her life easier, of course she was grieving, but she started drinking even more. Her behaviour became erratic and unacceptable. She would ask me over to help and then order me out of the kitchen, and would not allow me to eat any of the food that she had prepared, saying, "There wasn't enough for me and the customers!"

One day, we had a blazing row and she told me never to come back to the house. I didn't for three months, nor did I ring her. I was desperately sad and worried. Eventually, I wrote her a long letter expressing my concern and to try and rectify our separation.

Here is part of the content:

*"… when you become drunk you are a different person. The Alison I
gave birth to and watched grow into a beautiful girl and woman, is
no more. You were kind, understanding, sweet and sensitive and fun;
when drunk you become a critical, maudlin and impossible person.
Your beautiful face is now bloated and you are unhealthily thin. I love
you so much, which is why I have to tell you I think you need help. It
appears I cannot do that, but if you want to talk to me again, I am
here for you…"*

I then asked her if she would like to join me and some friends for dinner.
Ali rang me after receiving my letter; she did not apologise for her previous
behaviour, but agreed to join me for dinner. That evening she asked me to
come up to the yacht club during the week and have a talk, just the two of
us. I climbed the steps to the house again on the pre-arranged day and Ali
greeted me at the door with a smile, "Let's go in the back room, Mum, we
can be alone there."

Inside we sat on the sofa bed together and I held her fragile body in my
arms, as she broke down and wept.

"I am so sorry, Mum, I did not mean to hurt you. But I feel that I have a
hole in my heart that can never be filled, not by relationships, nor love from
you and my friends. I have a fear of not being good enough, an emptiness
inside, so I drink to try and forget my hollow heart."

"Darling Ali, you seem to have a fixation about being a middle child and
unloved, but I have told you frequently that I love you all in the same way. If
anything, you are probably closer to me than Fiona and Simon because we
both have this passion for Greece and we enjoy the same things and have
spent more time together. Whatever the fear is inside you, I think you have
to look at it, rather than cover it up with drinking. It may help to lighten your
mood with the first glass but it has been proven that drink is a depressant.
Please try to stop. Think of your father and what it did to him. As a child
you had a beautiful nature, which I'm sure you still posses, so try to find that
light again inside you and your emptiness will go away."

"Lizzie, you are my best friend, even though you talk a load of shit!" She
wiped the tears from her cheeks and kissed me. "I will try to stop." She did
for a couple of months, until we went to England for my son's wedding.

Simon had met a fellow student at Edinburgh University where he was studying for his Masters degree in Chemistry. Claire was a tall, pretty and intelligent girl and they had been living together for some time, so the marriage was not a surprise. Ali and I stayed with Fiona the night before driving up to Worcesteshire, where the ceremony was to be held in a beautiful Tudor mansion. I was putting Ali's holdall in the car when I noticed a bottle of vodka sticking out of the top of her bag. I removed it and put it back in the house.

It was a glorious sunny day and the reception was held on the lawns. Champagne was flowing and Simon and Claire looked deliriously happy as they wandered round greeting the guests and family. Fiona came up to me, "Ali's getting drunk, Mum, she's legless. I'm going to have a word."

I saw her steer Ali inside away from the crowd. Later they both emerged to join the photo session. Ali was standing beside me. She was a little contrite after the reprimand by her sister, but we still had dinner and dancing to enjoy. I went to bed after Simon and Claire had left for their honeymoon in Spain and noticed Ali still drinking at the bar.

"Time to stop, Ali," I whispered.

"Why? This is my brother's wedding, and I hope the only one – not like you!"

***

Next morning the housekeeper came up to me and said, "I hope your daughter is OK today; we had to put her to bed last night. She was a little worse for wear!"

I was ashamed that Ali had disgraced our family on Simon's special day and just hoped there were not too many people awake to see her being carried to her bedroom. Perhaps she had allowed herself to drink again for this special occasion and she would go back to sobriety in Greece.

2001 was a momentous year. America declared a war on terror after the horrifying Islamic terrorist attack on The World Trade Centre in New York on the 9th of September. Ali and I were having lunch at her favourite fish taverna by the sea on that tragic day. She went to the loo and as she was returning, she noticed the staff watching television. The screen showed a picture of burning skyscrapers. At first she thought it was a science fiction film, until she heard the commentary.

"Mum, come here quickly."

We gazed with disbelief as the towers crumbled to the ground and bodies hurtled from windows to try and escape the roaring fires. It was a sickening moment and the aftermath of the attack reverberated around the world. 2,996 people lost their lives and America vowed to find Bin Laden and stop Al-Qaeda from carrying out their threat to destroy the Western world. The struggle still continues.

Ali was forty years old that year. I arranged a party to be held on the mainland at a superb villa owned by my friends. It was easier for guests to come to a venue on the mainland than to go to Trizonia, where they would have to be reliant on water taxis to bring them back late at night. Simon and Fiona had flown over from England and close friends of Ali's stayed in the villa prior to the actual party night. Ali was in a sour mood: ungrateful that I had rented the villa and arranged for the food to be delivered (this was to give her a rest from cooking). She complained about all the arrangements until Simon, who is normally a calm and reasonable character, lost his temper and told her to behave!

The party was a huge success and ended with people skinny-dipping in the luxurious lit pool. Ali drank in moderation and even voiced her appreciation of my efforts on her behalf. I left the young ones dancing and swimming and fell into a contented long sleep. In the morning Simon and I had a chat. He was aware of Ali's excessive drinking and had told her she must try to stop. She had used the excuse that she was surrounded by drinkers every night; she did try for a month or a week at a time, but finally always succumbed.

"Perhaps you need to think about leaving the taverna and doing something else," Simon suggested.

"I wish," Ali had replied, "But I am committed, because of Bill. I can't let him down."

Fate, or destiny, or whatever you believe in, intervened to change her life.

FINALE

ACT XIII

I discovered the fascinating island of Lefkada in the Ionian Sea, when a friend took me there one weekend. It had white sandy beaches, a quaint small town and it was joined to the mainland by a causeway, so no need to get expensive ferries, and it was close to an airport where there were charter flights to England. I rented a cheap, small studio flat in the town centre. I had a small flat in Nafpaktos and would drive to Lefkada in three hours and swim in the glorious blue of the deserted beaches.

Ali was still running the yacht club, but every winter she would fly to Thailand where she would relax and forget the demands of the work in Trizonia. I saw her often when I was in Nafpaktos and helped her if she needed me. Her legs were worse; she had to wear support stockings to stop the swelling, which was unbearable in the heat. She would stop drinking for weeks at a time, then start again. One day I had a phone call from Ali.

"Mum, can you come over, I am not well."

I caught the next boat over to the island and found her sitting with her legs up on a stool.

"What is it, darling?"

"I was bitten in bed last night, by a centipede I think, and my legs are even more swollen."

At a glance I could see that her legs were red and swollen. I rang a doctor on the mainland. He said he would come over that night. I did what had to be done in the taverna whilst Ali rested, cooling her legs with ice packs. After examining Ali, the doctor said her condition was not serious. Often after a centipede bite there would be swelling and itching, but it would go away after a few days. Ali was not able to take penicillin, but he prescribed an antidote that she should take for a week and then see him again. He disappeared into the night to catch the last water taxi back to the mainland.

"This fucking island." I cried. "Centipedes in your bed, snakes in the roof, rats and mice everywhere, you have got to get away, Ali."

"Mum, calm down! I know there are disadvantages, but I love it here, you know that."

I stayed for a week until the swelling went down and helped as much as I could. Ali was a perfectionist and even in her fragile state she would not let me do all the cooking and cleaning, she said I was slovenly! I stayed in my flat in Nafpaktos to be near her because I knew she needed help, not only with the running of the taverna, but with the shopping and lifting.

One balmy spring day, a southerly wind blew a yacht into the bay and it moored below the house. The owners were a live- aboard couple from the Isle of Skye. Fiona and Geoff had taken time off from the harsh northern climate to explore the Mediterranean. Fiona had run a cafe in her local town and was also able to sew professionally. Geoff was a trained engineer and handyman. They came up to the yacht club and Ali liked them immediately. They agreed they would help Ali in the taverna with any jobs to be done if Fiona could bring her sewing machine up to the house and advertise her skill stitching sails and upholstery for any needy yachties. Also Fiona or Geoff would help with serving meals and Ali would pay them out of the proceeds. They were in no hurry to leave. Knowing Ali now had support, I returned to Lefkada.

I had a phone call from Ali in 2003. She was distraught; she poured out the gist of her problems. Bill had decided he wanted to sell the yacht club. He had owned it for over seven years and never made any money from it; he had let Ali live there and manage it without charging her much, but now he wanted to get his money back. He had a new girlfriend and they intended coming to Trizonia to refurbish the house. Ali would have to move out. "You know you can have my flat in Nafpaktos" I said, "I'm coming back to discuss what we can do in the future."

I felt desperately sorry for Ali who had built up the business and who loved the island, but I felt this would give her the impetus to start another career, one which would not be so arduous and bad for her health.

Bill and girlfriend, Hazel, closed the yacht club down. They stripped the insulation on the ceilings and found several snakes nesting; the rats and mice ran to the sea providing the feral cats with a feast. They slapped white paint everywhere and varnished the floors, then looked for a buyer.

Ali moved into my flat, tearful and furious.

"Lizzie, guess what? He has offered the taverna to a man I know. He is a charlatan and a wanker and he is known for not paying his debts, but he says he has cash! My friends on Trizonia know about his past and say they will not go to eat there, but I have an idea."

"Tell me, Ali."

"I will get a mortgage on my Surbiton flat and make Bill an offer!" This was not what I wanted to hear. I understood her feelings, the passion she had for the yacht club and Trizonia, which had been her home for thirteen years, but it was time for her to leave.

"Is that wise, darling? Can you pay the mortgage? Also consider the toll the work is taking on your legs. You won't get any better if you continue living and working there."

"Mum, this place feeds my soul and I believe living on Trizonia fills that hole in my heart; just to wake in the morning and be surrounded by nature's beauty makes me happy. I am passionate about this island."

Ali made an offer and Bill accepted; she moved back into the house and started business again. Fiona and Geoff had to leave, which meant Ali had to manage alone. However, a friend of Simon's came out in the summer to help with the serving and other friends arrived to give her support. In the winter she flew to Thailand. She visited doctors there to get advice about her increasingly swollen legs, none of them found a cure. They told her she lacked Vitamin K and she must not stand for long!

I had moved to Lefkada when I got a call from Daniel, Ali's friend, who was staying with her in Trizonia.

"Lizzie, I think you should come here. Ali was bleeding and I took her to the hospital in Patras; I am running the taverna for her."

I drove to the hospital immediately, but she had discharged herself and was back on the island. I found her lying on a bed looking pale and ill.

"What happened, darling?"

"I started to bleed internally, Mum, I think it's my colon. I have got fibroids, they told me in Bangkok. It was ghastly in the hospital; they left me in bloody sheets in the corridor and no one came to attend to me, so I left!"

Daniel had to return to America in a few days, so I stayed with her and kept the taverna open, but only served drinks and snacks. I insisted that she go to a private clinic in Patras. We closed the yacht club and I drove her to a modern, clean hospital where she had an examination. She was told that she had cysts in her colon and should have them removed. We booked her in for the operation. Ali stayed in the clinic for three days. The doctors removed the cysts and we were told they were not malignant.

Ali recovered from this operation, but her legs were swollen and covered in black bruises and pained her most of the time.

"Ali, you cannot manage anymore alone. Why not rent the yacht club until your legs are better. Go to Bangkok or England to get other opinions. It is madness to stay here in your condition."

Ali grudgingly admitted this could be an option. She advertised in an English paper and waited. Two men from the Channel Islands answered and came to view the property. They were very interested and said they would come back to her with their answer.

Ali struggled on.

In the summer of 2006 Ali met a man from Australia. He owned a yacht, was single and spent some time in the harbour in Trizonia. They planned to go sailing together. He did not drink and was a sensitive and thoughtful man who obviously adored Ali. She promised him she would go sailing with him, if she could rent the taverna. That winter she flew to Thailand. She could hardly walk and had to be assisted to the plane in a wheelchair. Ali spent Christmas alone in Bangkok; she visited more doctors, but had no positive suggestions about how to cure her legs.

In the new year of 2007, I met Ali at the bus station in Nafpaktos. She was looking better and was positive about the coming year, although still waiting for the reply about renting the taverna. She showed me what she had brought from Thailand, crammed into two suitcases.

"Look, Mum, if I come and live with you in Lefkada, I can sell these things in the street market."

There were silk cushion covers, dresses, and Thai jewellery. It seemed to me that she was considering leaving Trizonia at last. Ali also presented me with a gold pendant of Buddha. She had gone to an engraver and asked him to inscribe on the other side specific symbols that would bring me luck. She had visited Thailand so often, she became intrigued by the Buddhist philosophy and started to believe in its principles.

I drove her to Chania and we caught the water taxi across the sea to Trizonia, where Nicos was waiting with his tractor and trailer to cart us up the hill. Ali opened the front door and we peered into the kitchen and then the living room, wary of finding snakes. On the floor lay a dead white owl!

"Oh, Mum, the poor thing, it must have fallen down the chimney. It can't have been here for long, it's still warm."

I shivered as I picked the owl up and put it in a black bag to dispose of it outside.

Ali heard later that the couple who wanted to rent the yacht club were unable to do so, because the Channel Islands were not a member of the EU and they were therefore prevented from acquiring property to rent in Greece.

With her usual resilience, Ali reopened for the season. I knew she could not possibly manage alone, her legs were black with bruises and her hair had started to fall out. She had been proud of her thick gold locks, but she visited the hairdresser for a stylish short cut, which was necessary to stimulate new growth. With her artistic flair she decided to provide wedding parties at the taverna, using the incomparable view with the moon rising behind the mountains to attract romantic newlyweds. She had a few bookings and asked a local Greek girl, Viola to help her on those occasions.

I was glad to know she still had enthusiasm and energy to apply to her life, but one girl's help on rare occasions was not enough. I came up with a solution. I was letting one of my rooms in Lefkada to an Englishman called Rickie. He was an interior designer and scratched a living in Lefkada finding work wherever he could. He loved the Greek way of life and was fun and capable. I suggested to Rickie that he might like to work alongside Ali in Trizonia; Rickie was enthusiastic about the idea, so I asked Ali to come to Lefkada to meet him and discuss the prospect.

Ali came to stay with me for three days. She and Rickie liked each other and she told him what she expected of him in Trizonia and how much she could pay him. He agreed to the terms and was excited about a new adventure and seeing another island in Greece. In the daytime, Ali cycled around Lefkada or we swam together on the quiet sandy beaches, there was no one there to see her disfigured legs; we laughed and talked about the future with Rickie helping her in the yacht club.

"Lizzie, I have one wedding party at the weekend. I need to think about Rickie coming over. I will close the taverna after the party and rest. Then I will ring you with my decision."

"OK, darling. I will wait to hear from you on the Wednesday after the wedding party, and then we can decide when Rickie will come to Trizonia."

I was praying she would take advantage of this ideal solution and then she would always have someone there to help her and to watch over her. I was not the right person to be with her, she needed to separate from her mother.

When it was time for Ali to leave, I took her to the bus station in Lefkada. She had to change buses at Antirion, and then climb numerous steps to catch another bus to Nafpaktos, then get a taxi to Chania opposite Trizonia where she would need to get a water taxi to *her* island. After that, she would be taken to the house by Nicos in his tractor; she would have to climb down fifteen more steps to reach her house. I kissed her and waved goodbye to my free-spirited, wayward and unconventional daughter, my soul mate and my troubled middle child.

Rickie plied me with questions about Trizonia. I told him of the island's natural beauty, but also emphasised the difficulties in reaching the house when bringing supplies from the mainland; I mentioned how solitary it could be and that, if there were no customers, you would be without any human contact for several days.

On Wednesday I rang Ali, as we had agreed. There was no reply on her main line house phone. I tried her mobile, but it was switched off. I thought she was probably resting and sleeping, so I tried to send her an email, but the Internet connection was not working. Ali did not ring me that day. On Thursday, I tried again – still no reply from either of her phones, nor did Ali ring. By Friday my intuition told me something was wrong. I rang Viola, the Greek girl who lived on the island, and asked her to go up to the yacht club to check that Ali was all right. Viola said she would walk up later in the afternoon.

In the early evening I received an incoherent call from Viola. She did not speak any English and my Greek was not perfect.

"Lizzie, Ali is in hospital in Patras."

"Why? What is the matter with her?" I asked.

"I think you should go to Patras now."

I could get no more sense from her and the language was a barrier, so I rang a mutual Greek friend of ours, Demitri, who spoke fluent English, as he was working in Patras.

"Demitri, can you please ring the hospital and find out what is the matter with Ali. I can't understand what Viola is trying to tell me."

"Of course, Lizzie, I'll ring straight away."

I was alone in my flat. I tried to keep calm, but could not. I paced up and down until the phone rang: it was Demitri.

"Lizzie, sit down, have a glass of whisky or something. I have to tell you that Ali is dead!"

"No!" I screamed. "It's not possible! How? Why?"

"I will explain later, Lizzie. I am coming over to see you and I will bring Poli (my best Greek girlfriend who lived in Patras), but now you must have someone with you in Lefkada."

It took three hours to drive from Patras.

I was in shock. I did not cry. I poured myself an ouzo, and then another, in the vain hope that the alcohol would stop the pain in my heart, that it was a bad dream and Ali was still alive. Then the phone rang again. It was the consul from the British Embassy. He knew Ali was dead and was in the mortuary in Patras Hospital, and he would be at my flat in the morning to discuss arrangements for her funeral.

It was true –my daughter was dead.

I always thought that if one of my children died, I would die too, but I didn't. I rang Fiona in England, she was due to fly out to Lefkada on Sunday for a holiday; I told her the unbelievable news of her sister's death. Fiona tried to be calm; she heard the tremor in my voice and knew she had to be strong for me.

"I will tell Simon, Mum, you don't have to ring him. I will try and get him on the same flight this Sunday."

The brain is an incredible instrument. I managed to shut out the horror of Ali's death and continued carrying out normal tasks, albeit like an automaton, until Demitri, Poli and Rickie arrived to be with me. Poli lit candles, Demitri poured more drinks, Rickie made me a sandwich, and then they put me to bed. I slept in a drunken stupor until next morning.

The man from the British Consulate arrived early. He was sympathetic and efficient and explained there were certain procedures to be carried out. I had to go to the police station opposite Trizonia to collect Ali's personal belongings and to sign papers and the death certificate. This had to be done today. It was a four-hour drive and I was not able to think, let alone drive. Ricki was with me and offered to take me there.

"How did she die?" I asked the consul.

"Alison had an aortic aneurism." He replied. "It would have been very quick and she would not have felt any pain."

"She was alone when she died?"

"Yes. I am afraid she had been dead for three days before she was found."

My intuition was correct. I was screaming inside. My Ali died on her own. I had not been there to help her, to comfort her, to know if she had been frightened or in pain. Feelings of guilt swamped me and I started to cry for the first time.

Ricki hugged me until my tears subsided.

"Darling Lizzie, we have to go. Be brave."

I remember nothing of the long drive. We were met at the police station by a sorrowful Viola. I thanked her for all she had done. It must have been a fearful shock for her to find Ali dead and then to arrange for Ali's body to be transported from the island to hospital.

The police were kind. They suggested a good undertaker for Ali's funeral. There was no cremation in Greece at that time, so it was assumed she would be buried. I nodded and left with Ali's passport and wallet. Those items were all that were left of her.

Viola, Ricki and I went for a coffee. Viola explained her shocking discovery on that tragic day. She had gone to the house, and as she could not get in through the door, she went round to the side window, which had a view of the interior back room. Ali was lying on the bed; she had her dressing gown on and her atomizer was lying on the floor beside her. Viola broke the window open, climbed in and realised Ali was dead. Viola rang the police who came very quickly and took Ali's body on a stretcher, down to the village, on to a water taxi, and then to Patras Hospital. Viola did not know how to tell me that Ali was dead, which is why she told me to go to the hospital where Ali was in the mortuary. We cried together as we said goodbye and I told her I would be in touch when the funeral arrangements had been made.

I woke on Sunday morning. The terrible realisation of Ali's death hit me. It is like that every morning – something is wrong – the knowledge that I will no longer see her again leaves me bereft. I struggle to face the day. I drove to Preveza airport to meet Fiona and Simon. They encircled me with their arms and I saw the sorrow in their eyes, they had to acknowledge we were now a family of only three. I explained the tragic circumstances of Ali's death as we returned to my flat. Simon took over the practical arrangements; it was his way of avoiding the pain he felt. He sent emails to all of Ali's friends, informing them of her death.

We sat together trying to decide on the practical issues we had to carry out. God, how wonderful it was to have them with me, my two remaining children who knew and understood their unconventional sister. Ali was in the mortuary and we needed to arrange with the consul what we wanted to do with her body. We went to the local cemetery and wandered round. It was large and there was no sense of tranquillity.

"Ali would not want to be buried here," Fiona said. "She told me she wanted to be cremated anyway."

"There is no cremation in Greece." I replied.

"We must talk to the consul," Simon said. We found out that we could fly Ali's body to England. There an undertaker could keep her body until we got back and she could be cremated, as she had wished.

The cost was huge, £7,000. I didn't care. I had exactly that amount in the Northern Rock Building Society (I had been advised to leave money there for emergencies by an accountant friend). We told the consul to make the arrangements. I wanted Ali's body to be at rest. Within a week of my decision and payment, the Northern Rock Building Society collapsed!

The replies to Simon's emails were overwhelming. Condolences came from all over the world. I knew that Ali's Internet connection was not working before she died, so she had phoned many of her friends in Australia. It was as though she had an intuition that she might not speak to them again. Serendipitously her beloved friend, Daniel, was in Greece, not in America. He arrived on the bus from Athens and we held each other.

"I cannot believe it, Lizzie, she was my greatest friend. I loved her despite her faults; she was loyal, generous, funny and totally original. I can never replace the relationship we had together."

The proof of Ali's strong friendships was the arrival of another friend, Laura, from England. She had met Ali in Trizonia when she and her husband Tom had sailed into the island and stayed to help Ali in the yacht club. I asked Laura why she had flown over?

"What else could I have done, Lizzie?" she replied.

I loved her for her simple response and the knowledge that she cared for Ali so much that she needed to be with me to say goodbye.

Simon sent out invitations to the wake. We were to assemble in my flat and arranged for Simon, Fiona, Laura, Daniel and me to make short speeches, then we would walk up to a taverna nearby for food and drink. Flowers and wreaths were delivered to my flat, hundreds of tokens from friends who loved Ali. As we walked up to the taverna for the meal, I noticed many fireflies or glowworms in the bushes surrounding my flat. Lighting our way and a reminder that Ali's light was still burning – somewhere above me.

The practicalities of booking flights back to England, arranging for an undertaker and the other funeral arrangements in the UK were dealt with by Fiona and Simon. I was still in shock; my friends did what they could to help, but I was living a half-life. I read through the emails from Ali's friends and there was one that touched me more than any other. It was from a French man, Pasqual; he was responsible for the maintenance of a seismometer recording station on Trizonia and would check it three times a year. The words he wrote epitomise Alison's qualities:

"I remember working quite late in the evening and then walking up the dark track, tired, dried out by the wind and sun or hit by cold and lashing rain and feeling worried about the taverna being closed, but then feeling relieved when, arriving at the little gate at the bottom of the steps, I heard the chatter of guests up there – my shelter. This was certainly my greatest pleasure in Trizonia: enjoying Alison's delicious food, the peace of the place, the soft music and, overall, to stay after supper talking with her for hours over a bottle of wine. Often I was introduced to other visitors who came, just like me, to this harbour above a harbour."

"Alison's taverna," he continued, *"offered something quite extraordinary which I will always remember: a mixture of joy and melancholy. Alison's dream world, which she was able to recreate every evening for her visitors, a world which I knew, was also a difficult world. I guess her health suffered a lot from this uneasy life. She was charming, clever, gentle, interested in peoples' souls and I will remember her warm welcome and her kindness. I will always keep her memory in my heart."*

Ali's funeral was held at Leatherhead Crematorium, a leafy suburban setting in Surrey. Family and many of her friends from England arrived to say goodbye. Simon and I made short tributes. These were the words I found to convey how I felt:

"A man who has lost a wife is called a widower,
A woman who has lost a husband is called a widow,
A child who has lost its parents is called an orphan,
But, there is no word for a parent who has lost a child; that is how
terrible the loss is."

The white coffin was bedecked with flowers. My daughter was inside that casket; I had asked the undertaker if I could see her before the final service, but he advised against it. Of course, I understood. My child had been transported from place to place, from one country to another over a period of two weeks; she was no longer the beautiful Ali I had known. The indescribable horror and knowledge of the finality of her life hit me when I watched the white coffin slide through the curtains into the furnace of the crematorium.

We collected her ashes (they were in a wooden box) and Fiona, Simon and I knew what we had to do with them – we had to take them back to Trizonia. Fiona and I and two of Ali's greatest friends flew to Athens and then travelled on to Trizonia. The empty house stared at us, as though questioning where its owner was.

We took her ashes down the steep steps to the jetty below and scattered them into the clear blue sea – but they would not wash away and they stayed beside the shore. Ali did not want to leave her home. Slowly the wind changed and her ashes gradually flowed with the current into the sea that surrounded her island and which gave her endless pleasure during the years she lived there. I knew her soul lived on.

We sat together on the balcony reminiscing about Ali, suddenly a colourful butterfly settled on Fiona's nose; it stayed there for a long time then flew into the sky. I remembered that the Greeks believe a butterfly, or *petaloutha*, represents the soul of the dead. So, swiftly, Ali had come to say hello to us and to let us know she was on her way to nirvana.

I had loved Trizonia as Ali had, but I had this inexplicable feeling of a darkness surrounding the place. A Greek friend of mine, who lived in the area, and was a water diviner, had told me that there were adverse lei lines running through the island. Within the 500 metres area surrounding our house, four people had tragically died; two Greek people in the houses next door and a frenchwoman in the house above us, and now Ali. How to explain this? I know not. I was glad I left when I did.

I found Ali's unsigned will; because I am her mother everything was left to me – her flat in Surbiton and the yacht club in Trizonia – and for the first time in my life I did not have to worry about money. I would have given it all back to have Ali alive again. It was her last gift to me. It took two years to sell the yacht club. Every time I returned to show prospective buyers the house, I was overwhelmed with memories and struggled to find the right words which would attract a new owner; I only wanted Ali there, standing at the door wearing the badge I gave her, stating: "*Actually, I'm Alison.*"

I had experienced the death of many loved ones before, but how was I to cope with my daughter of forty-five predeceasing me? My pain was indescribable! No longer would I hear her raucous laugh, see her wide smile or feel her touch, I wanted to scream,

"Come back, Ali. Let me at least say goodbye."

I found some consolation in a book called *The Tibetan Book of Living and Dying*. I found the Buddhist explanation of the stages a person goes through, after death and then their eventual re-birth, helpful and pacifying. I was interested to know that Buddhists believe that a body should not be touched for three days, so that the soul can be at peace. Ali was dead for three days before she was found. There was so much wisdom in the book, which helped me bear the pain I was feeling. A quote from Rumi was one that was enlightening: "Grief can be the garden of compassion". If you keep your heart open through everything, your pain can become your greatest ally in your life's search for love and wisdom.

Then I discovered another book that answered my continual questioning about an afterlife, it was called *The Journey of Souls*, written by a Dr Michael Newton. He is a hypnotherapist and had noticed that while patients were under hypnosis, they had conversations with the dead, usually with someone they loved. Dr Newton recorded all the conversations (with the patients' approval) and his published accounts prove there is a place in infinity where souls gather in groups to prepare for an afterlife.

This revelation gave me the courage to continue my life with the knowledge that, at my death, I would see Ali again. I have learnt to be more compassionate and I always talk to those who have been recently bereaved, because I know they want to talk about their loss. The pain of my loss stays within me. It comes in waves; some days they are huge seventy foot waves, on other days they are smaller. I will never forget my daughter. I now have a hole in my heart that I cannot fill. When I see a butterfly I welcome it, believing it could be Ali or Ronnie's soul, letting me know they are at peace.

It is nine years since Ali died, but the knowledge that I still have Fiona and Simon to share my life with has helped me to be more optimistic. They are loving and caring and involve me in their lives and plans. I have two grandchildren, Simon's sons, who are my greatest joy. Ben and Joe are growing into clever, thoughtful and kind young men. I watch their development with interest and wonder what the future holds for them. They are fortunate to have two parents so, hopefully, will not experience the loss of a father as Fiona and Simon did. I am proud of my remaining family and pray they will have a more stable life than I was able to provide.

Well, that was my destiny – perhaps their stars have mapped an easier time for them all whilst on this earth.

EPILOGUE

"... when [she] shall die
Take [her] and cut [her] out in little stars
And [she] will make the face of heaven so fine
That all the world will be in love with night
And pay no worship to the garish sun..."

W. Shakespeare, *Romeo and Juliet*